THE
BEAD BOOK

THE
BEAD BOOK

Create your own beautiful beadwork

Sara Withers

CHARTWELL
BOOKS, INC.

A QUINTET BOOK

Published by Chartwell Books
A Division of Book Sales, Inc.
114 Northfield Avenue
Edison, New Jersey 08837

This edition produced for sale in the U.S.A.,
its territories and dependencies only.

ISBN 0-7858-0311-4
Reprinted 2004
This book was designed and produced by
Quintet Publishing Limited
6 Blundell Street
London N7 9BH

CREATIVE DIRECTOR: *Richard Dewing*
DESIGNER: *Simon Balley*
PROJECT EDITOR: *Diana Steedman*
EDITOR: *Karin Fancett*
PHOTOGRAPHER: *Paul Forrester*

Typeset in Great Britain by
Central Southern Typesetters, Eastbourne
Manufactured by Regent Publishing Services Ltd, Hong Kong
Printed by SNP Leefung Printing Limited, China

introduction

~

Over the last few years, many of us appear to have gone a little "bead crazy". In the United States you can now buy T-shirts emblazoned with the words "Bead Addict", or fabrics that are patterned with bead designs. There are many retail, mail-order, and wholesale suppliers of beads, a company that specializes in bead parties for children, and any number of bead societies, fairs and

symposiums. Perhaps the idea that Manhattan was bought for a handful of beads is a myth – but the bead trading tradition is flourishing in America, and in other parts of the world. Britain has a large number of beadworkers, a thriving bead society and internationally important bead businesses. This seems to be repeated in many parts of the world, lots of new beads are being produced, dying arts are being revived and many old beads are being traded.

With this abundance of old and new beads in evidence, what can you make with them? In *Creative Bead Jewellery* we have tried to illustrate a wide spectrum of the beads that are available and items that you can make with them. The jewellery designs range from classic "pearl" chokers to necklaces of brightly coloured wooden beads used with rubber tubing. Many of the necklaces have matching ear-rings too.

uction

There are also ideas for presents, clothing and items that can be used for interior decoration. The aim is to inspire you – the projects can be copied exactly or adapted for use with beads that you have already. Some of the beads used in the book are easier to buy in the United States and some are more readily available in Europe, so make the most of what you can get and enjoy being adaptable. We hope that the ideas in the book will inspire you and that you will soon learn to add your own identity to them.

buying beads

In the introduction we have already mentioned some of the places where you can buy beads, but here we give more details of possible suppliers.

First, there are bead stores. Many cities have a specialist bead shop, or perhaps a craft supply store that sells a selection of beads. This, of course, is where you would have the greatest variety to choose from, and it is very nice to be able to actually see the colors and shapes before you commit yourself. It also gives you the opportunity to try looking at

different beads together to see if they really will compliment each other. Some department stores now have a selection of beads in their notions department; if you are keen on doing beadwork or embroidery with rocaille beads, this is often a good source.

Second, you can buy by mail order, as there are now a host of useful catalogs available, mainly with good color photography, which makes buying easy. The disadvantage of mail order is the frustration of waiting for your order to come when you have a project ready in your mind, and the acute frustration of items sometimes being out of stock when you have carefully chosen them. This having been said, the bead catalogs are invaluable if you live in a remote area, and they provide a wonderful selection.

What other sources are there? Antique markets will sometimes have damaged necklaces that can be re-made, and thrift shops often have strings of beads that you can re-use with other beads. Ethnic stores usually have some beads that come from the countries that they are dealing with, and flea markets are another possible source. Do not forget to keep an eye out for beads when you are on vacation; although most countries export their beads to the United States and Europe, it is exciting to find them yourself. Finally, in some areas people are organizing bead parties in their homes, so it is a good idea to be aware of anything like that near you.

Beads are made from many different materials: ceramics, glass, wood, plastic, and bone, and more expensive materials including semi-precious stones such as malachite and lapis lazuli. The list is extensive, and in addition you should remember that you can make beads from yourself from materials like polymer clays, paper, air-dried clay, etc.

Most aspects of buying beads are a question of common sense. Think of their condition and check them for cracks or rough edges. Think carefully about the size of the holes in relation to the threads that you want to use: nowadays some beads like the Peruvian clay beads are made in the same designs with either large holes for leather or small holes for thread. Think about the types of beads that you are using together; it would be unwise to put very delicate beads between very heavy beads. Be aware of colorfastness: some brightly colored wooden beads, for example, are susceptible to losing their color. The content of metal beads needs consideration; some ethnic metal beads are either "white metal" or low-grade silver, whereas others can be very high-grade silver and can compare with sterling silver. If you are using semiprecious stone beads, or expensive glass beads, it is sensible to put high-grade silver with them, if possible. High-grade silver beads are likely to be priced by weight rather than per bead, although this is not a strict rule. There are also many beads available that are made from metallized plastic; these have a huge variety of good designs, and seem to be very durable.

Most beads are sized in millimeters (mm) with reference to their diameter (6 mm spheres) or length times diameter (15 x 4 mm tubes). The main exception to this is rocaille beads, which are the small glass beads, also known as seed beads, or sometimes pound beads, which are

used for bead weaving, bead embroidery, and with bead looms. They are sized by number – usually from 0/11, which are the smallest, to 0/6, which are the largest. However, the sizing does vary according to the manufacturer and can be reversed (i.e. 7/0); the basic guide is that the higher numbers are smaller sizes. Other beads often used in bead weaving,

embroidery, etc., are bugles; these are small glass tubes, which come in sizes 4″ (or 4″), which are the largest, to 1″, which is the smallest (the size does not refer to inches!).

You will quickly learn the sorts of beads that you enjoy working with; some people only work with tiny beads, many others say that they do not have the patience to use small beads, but will spend endless hours threading large dramatic beads. Do not forget, as you are hunting for your beads, that older beads represent a lot of history and are very collectible. In the same way, some of the beads that are being made now will be collectible in the future.

equipment and techniques

Round-nose pliers

When you start to work with beads, you can manage with very few tools. Scissors and pliers are the main necessity. Pliers are really a question of personal choice. If you are making a lot of straight earrings, then a small pair of *round-nose pliers* is essential, and it is advisable to use pliers with short "noses," as long ones make your work seem remote. Again, if you are going to do a lot of work with wires, (eyepins, headpins, or using jewelry wire), then a pair of *wirecutters* or snips will make the work easier.

Many of the necklaces in the projects are finished with french crimps or calottes, and you will need pliers to work with these. Once again it is a question of personal taste; *flat-nose pliers* are often used but, as you will see from the step by step instructions, we have used *sprung round-nose pliers* for this work. Some people find them more awkward, but they are often more powerful – because of this discrepancy, the projects refer to necklace pliers, and leave the choice to you.

You will also need a selection of *needles*, very fine ones if you are working with tiny beads (long thin beading needles are excellent for loom work), and blunt large-eyed needles will help with larger beads.

Wire cutters

If you are going to do wirework, then a *fine file* will be essential. Likewise if you do a lot of knotting or weaving, fine *tweezers* will be useful. This leads to the subject of *looms*. The most readily available bead looms are metal, but they can be quite difficult to use and probably have deterred many people from this sort of beadwork. If you feel that you will have the patience to work with tiny beads, then it would be advisable to buy a wooden loom, which will make your work very much more enjoyable.

Flat-nose pliers

Beading needles

It is useful to have some fast-acting *glue* on hand. It should never be allowed to dry beside good beads, as it will ruin them, but can be used in projects using inexpensive beads to decorative effect. It is also very effective for making sure knots stay tight.

You will need something to measure with, and having a mirror close to your work surface is often helpful. Finally, do not forget that good lights are a most important part of your basic equipment.

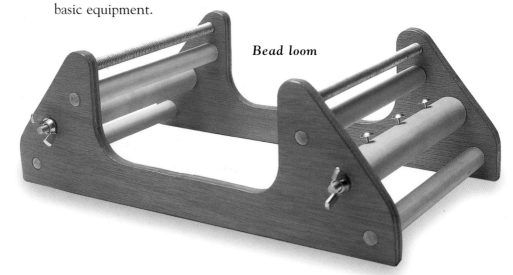

Bead loom

threads

Leather thonging

You have got your tools and your beads organized, and now it is time to consider what you will put them onto. The easiest threading material is *leather*, and a few beads with large holes, of course, put onto a thong, with some knots to finish it, can look stunning. The next material to consider is *nylon monofilament* (or fishing line, which is basically the same thing). This should be used with caution (some people say that it should never be used!), as it cannot be effectively knotted, so must be used with French crimps or calottes, and it produces stiff results that do not hang very well. It also has a tendency to shrink, so if you use it, it is advisable to leave a small gap between your beads and fastener to allow for this. The advantage of nylon monofilament is that it has a rigid end for threading, will not fray, and is strong, so it is good for chokers or bracelets that do not need to hang well. It is also a good material for children to work with.

Tiger tail (or soft line) is another good strong threading material, made of wire with a plastic coating. It is excellent for use with heavy beads, but be careful when working with it, as it does not forget any kinks that are made in it, and can snap where it has been kinked. It is best to finish tiger tail with French crimps.

Nylon monofilament

Tiger tail

Actual threads are often made of polyester or similar manmade fibers. In this book we have mainly used a *thick polyester whipping twine* for heavy beads, or a *fine polyester thread* for small beads. Both of these are very strong and durable, and the thick one comes in several colors and can be supplied with a waxed finish, which makes it possible to use without a needle. This thread is ideal for knotting, plaiting, and braiding, and can be used with calottes and French crimps. It hangs nicely and is ideal for most beads, as long as they do not have very small holes. However, if you use it with very heavy beads, it makes sense to allow your necklace to hang for a few days before you finish the ends, as the thread stretches to a certain extent. The thin polyester is also very strong and is excellent for weaving, loomwork, or other use with small beads, and again it can be finished in many different ways.

Polyester thread

There are other synthetic threads on the market, all of which can be very useful. Another possibility is *silk thread*. This is mostly sold on cards, with an integral needle which is extremely helpful. Silk comes in lots of different colors and some different thicknesses, and again is extremely strong and hangs beautifully. The only drawback to it is that it is expensive.

In addition to the threads that we have mentioned, do not forget that there are many beautiful *linen threads*, exciting cords, and of course, *chains* to be used. Once again, use your imagination, and, as you become confident with the techniques, you will be able to use all sorts of materials.

Silk thread

findings

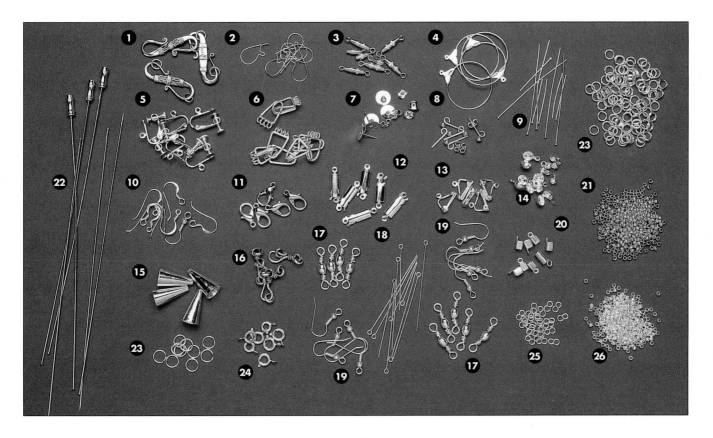

These are the mysterious bits that hold everything together for you!

We will start with earrings. Straight earrings are threaded onto *eyepins* or *headpins*, both of which come in different lengths and in different finishes. Both are efficient, but eyepins have more versatility. To hang earrings, you need either *screw* or *clip fittings* for unpierced ears, or *earwires* for pierced ears. The most common earwires are *hook* (or *fishhook*) wires, *kidney wires,* and *earstuds with hook*; the last type has a *friction nut* or *scroll* behind the ear. The names by which they are sold can

key

1	Hooks with jump rings	**15**	Cones
2	Kidney wires	**16**	Hooks with jump rings
3	Screw clasps	**17**	Swivels
4	Hoops	**18**	Eyepins
5	Screw/clip earwires	**19**	Earwires (fish hook)
6	Triple spacer clasps	**20**	Leather (or lace)
7	Earstud and nut		end crimps
8	Earstud with loop	**21**	French crimps (gilt)
9	Headpins	**22**	Hat pins with
10	Earwires (sterling silver)		safety ends
11	Trigger clasps	**23**	Jump rings
12	Spring clasps	**24**	Bolt rings
13	Earclips	**25**	Figure-eights
14	Calottes	**26**	French crimps
			(silver-plated)

vary slightly, as you can see. Flat *earstuds* or *earclips* are what you need to make plain stud earrings. All the earring findings that have been mentioned are available in silver plate, gilt plate, sterling silver, and gold. Although for most people it is quite acceptable to use plated metals for the hanging parts of the earrings, it is advisable to buy the pure metals to go through the ears. Gold is expensive (but at least if you are making your own earrings you can re-use the findings), whereas sterling silver is usually very reasonably priced. However, some people can only tolerate gold, while some can only tolerate silver.

There are other findings that relate to earrings. For example, you can buy lots of different hangers that can add to the scope of your designs, and you can buy ready-made hoops to which you can add beads.

For necklaces there is another set of findings. *Clasps* or *fasteners* come in many varieties, with *bolt rings* (which are used with *jump rings*) perhaps the most conventional. There are also *screw clasps, torpedo clasps,* and *box clasps,* to name but a few. The box clasps often come with loops for two or three-strand necklaces, and plain *sprung box clasps* are very reliable as they seldom work loose. You can also buy beautiful fasteners that will be an integral part of your design (such as in the "triple pearl choker"). Do not forget that you can also buy attractive *hooks* and *rings,* or you can make them yourself. Most people will tolerate plated fasteners, but again there are a few people who have to wear pure metals.

Unless you use knots, you will need to attach your fasteners with *French crimps* or *calottes,* which come in different sizes. Leather or cord necklaces can be finished with *spring ends* or *leather crimps* (also called *lace end crimps*) and then a hook.

That covers the more basic findings for you, but if you go into a bead shop, or open a good catalog, you will find a wealth of *spacer bars, cones* for multistrand necklaces, *dropper hangers* for the ends of elaborate multistrand necklaces, *bead tips*, etc. As you grow more confident, you will have the pleasure of trying them.

However, before we finish this section, there are a few other findings that should be mentioned including *figure-eight findings*, which are tiny pieces that change the way things hang, and *split rings*, which are more fiddly to use than jump rings, but safer. You can buy long pins with safety ends meant for *hatpins*, but you can cut them down if you are making long earrings with heavy beads. Do not forget about brooches. You could, for example, glue beautiful beads to *brooch backs*, or you might painstakingly thread small beads onto headpins and then into a perforated finding to create lovely brooches or earrings.

Not quite in the category of findings, but important to mention at this stage, is jewelry wire. This can be bought in different gauges, and in different finishes, i.e. silver-plated, brass, etc. Getting used to using wire opens up new horizons in your work. In the book we have shown you how to wire "donuts" and to make your own hooks and jump rings. All good findings suppliers will also supply wire, and it makes sense to explore the possibilities.

Silver wires

The great advantage of making jewellery with beads is that you can use fairly simple techniques in different situations and build your work. As we have illustrated in the book, once you have mastered the basic techniques, you can use them in lots of different situations and produce very satisfying results. Start with the basics – the first photograph shows you how to hold your pliers so that your control is good. To make a *loop*, hold your eyepin or headpin between your finger and thumb, using the other fingers to control it

wiring

as well. You need about ⅜ in (8 mm) of wire to make the loop. To make the headpin or eyepin the right length for the loop, either clip off any excess with wirecutters, or "fatigue" the wire by putting your pliers on each side of it and gently moving the wire back and forth until the metal breaks cleanly. Put your round-nose pliers around the wire above your beads. Bring the wire toward you so that it is at an angle of 45 degrees from the straight piece, then move the pliers to the top of the wire and roll the wire away from you around the pliers. You do not have to do it in one movement. If you have not made a complete circle, take your pliers out and make the movement again, until you have a neat loop. If you then want to connect this loop into another one, for example to make a double-length earring, open the loop sideways with your pliers, so that you do not damage the metal. The same applies to attaching an earwire; open the loop on the earwire sideways and add the loop on your eyepin or headpin.

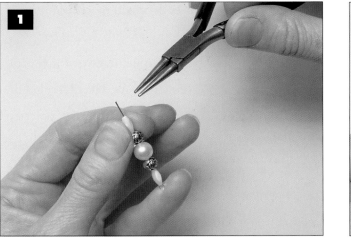

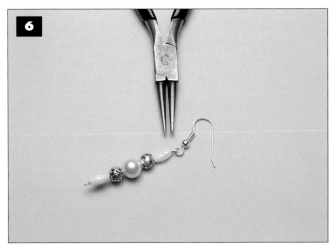

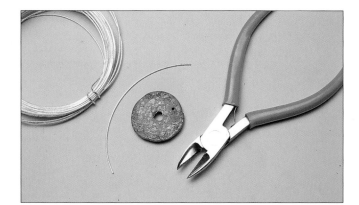

You can, of course, do much more than just roll loops if you are using jewelry wire. It can be incorporated in your designs in many ways. Brass wire is rather springy and is harder to use, but silverplated wire is easier to manage, especially after some practice. Choose 0.8 wire for making decorative coils, or to wire a "donut" and 1.2 wire if you need something more rigid like a hook or a jump ring. It is hard to give precise measurements for wire work, as the items that you are planning to use will vary. The wire is not expensive, so it is best to cut a piece of wire, keep a record of its length, and then practice and experiment.

To *wire a "donut"* or something similar, cut your wire in similar proportions to those shown in the photograph. Fold the wire through the "donut," leaving one end longer than the other. Roll the short end to make a loop. Then wrap the longer end around the bottom of the loop. Keep wrapping this wire until you have several neat coils, then clip the end, and gently press the top coil in with your pliers to make it neat.

To wire a "donut"

1

2

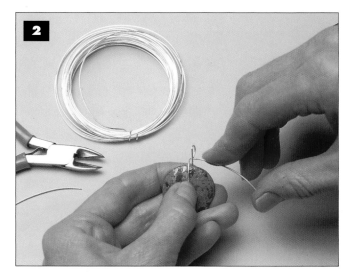

To make a jump ring

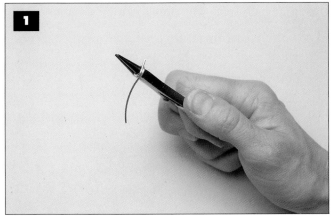

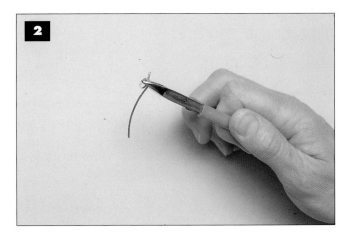

A *jump ring* can be made to match by rolling the wire around your pliers, or something else round, then clipping through the circles, and moving the ends together.

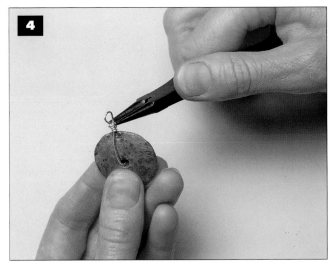

If you are threading beads onto wire and you want a more *elaborate and secure loop* at the top of them, try the following. Bring your wire up, make a loop allowing extra wire, then wrap the extra wire under the loop. Again make several coils and press the end in neatly.

To make a *hook*, cut a few millimeters of wire, then file one end and turn a loop in this end. Now curve the wire back around your pliers, clip off any excess wire, bend up the end of this wire to make a good shape, and file this end, too.

To make a hook

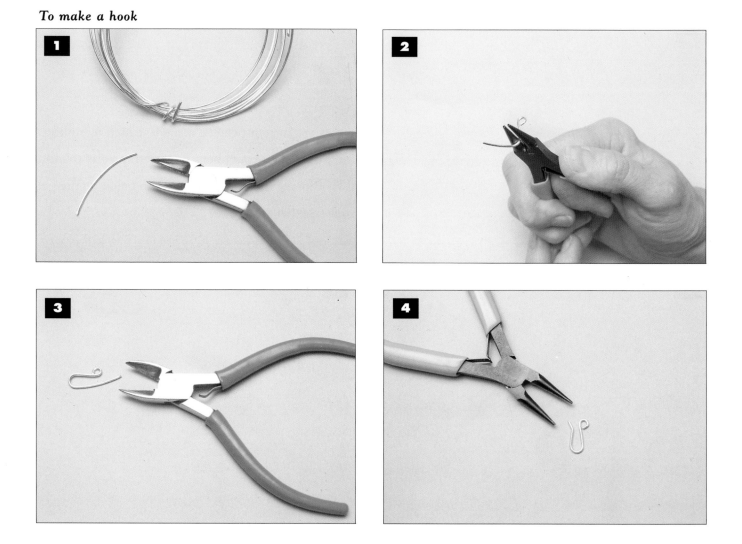

finishing

Leather or cotton thonging can be finished either with knots, or with *spring ends* or *lace end crimps*. Spring ends look like coils of wire, and you fit them to your thong and press the last coil into the leather with your pliers. The lace end crimps are folded around the thong from either side and squeezed with your pliers.

The simplest way to finish a necklace or bracelet is by crimping

Spring clasps

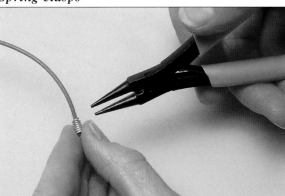

Lace end crimps

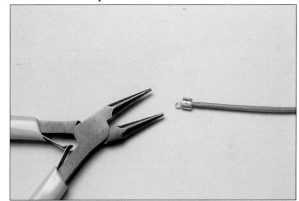

the ends with French crimps. In the threads section we discussed which threads are suitable for crimping. To do this, simply put one or two of the crimps onto the thread that you are using (in this case tiger tail), fold the thread through your fastener, and back through the crimps. Make sure that your crimps are close to your beads (except on fishing line, which shrinks a little) and that your loop is neat but allows movement, and then squeeze the crimps firmly with your pliers. Make sure that the crimps will not move on your thread, but do not squeeze so firmly that

French crimps

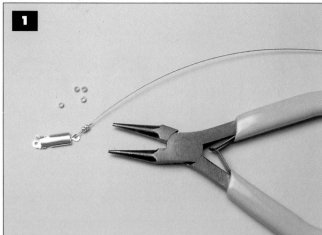

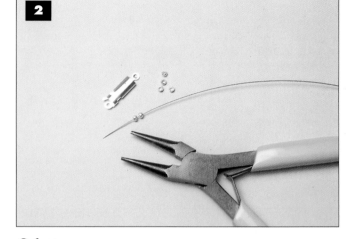

Calottes

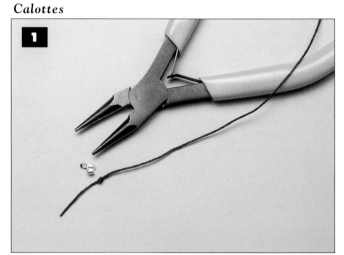

you damage the thread.

Another easy way to finish a necklace is to knot the thread (again we have discussed which threads are suitable), and then squeeze a *calotte* over the knot and attach your fastener to the calotte. You can put a drop of glue onto the knot before you cover it with the calotte, for extra safety, but make sure that the glue does not touch and spoil any precious beads. When you squeeze the calotte again, make sure that you do not damage the thread.

Knots should be explained at this point. If you are finishing with a knot and calotte, or using a knot at the end of a tassel, and want to

To knot between beads

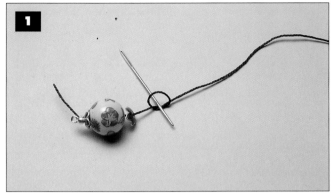

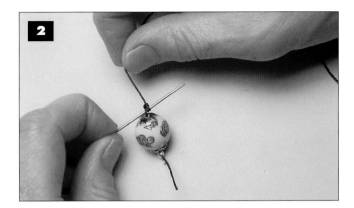

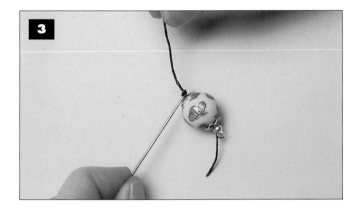

To make a double knot

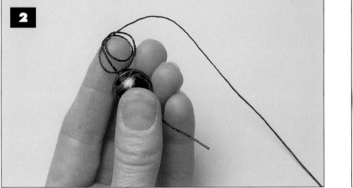

make sure that the knot is close to your beads, put a needle into the knot before you tighten it, then draw the knot back toward the beads with the needle and gently pull the needle out when the knot is sitting next to the beads. *To knot between beads*, you need to allow approximately twice as much thread as the length of your finished necklace. The length needed, of

AQM

course, is dependent on the size of your beads and the number of knots, and you should allow even more thread if you are going to have a lot of knots, as it is easier to cut off the excess than to have to reknot due to lack of thread. Use a needle in the knots between beads in the same way as before, so that all your spacing is even. If your beads have larger holes, you can make double knots to go between them.

Knots are another appropriate way of finishing a necklace and *attaching a fastener*. To do this, make a single knot next to your beads, and leave a needle in it. Put on your fastener, leaving space for more knots between it and the knot with the needle in it. Then put the knots into

Attaching a fastener

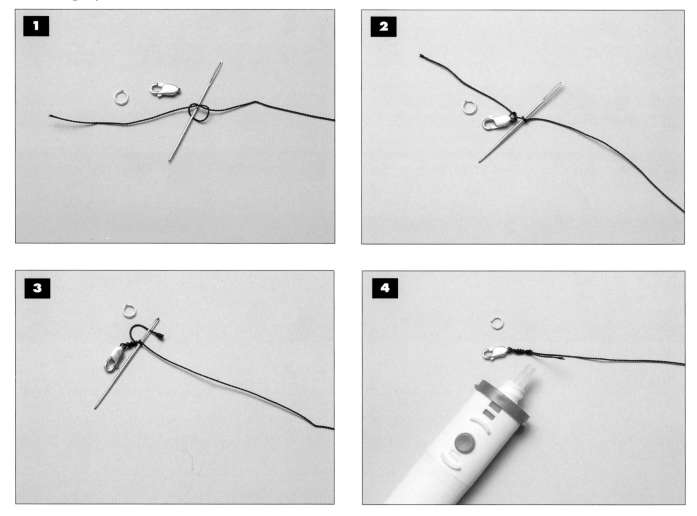

this space, remembering how many you have used, and how much space you left, so that you can duplicate on the other side. When you have made these knots, put your thread into the needle that you left in the knot, and pull the needle through to tighten everything. Either put a drop of glue onto the last knot and cut off your loose thread, or if you have large enough holes, thread it back into your beads.

If you have a few special beads, another way to finish them is to braid the ends. The technique that we have used is a simple macrame technique. You need three strands, either single or double. When your strands are ready, leave the middle one in place and work the left-hand

Finishing a multi-strand necklace

strand under the middle and over the right-hand strand. Work the right-hand strand over the middle and under the left-hand strand. Continue in this way as the braid builds. You can knot the ends or add a fastener, and braid back over the ends that attach the fastener.

Braiding is one good way to finish a multistrand necklace. Another way to do this is to make loops with crimps at each of the ends, and then pass another thread with a loop at the end through these loops and back into itself. Put a bell cap or a cone over all the ends, and either thread more beads onto the single string, or finish on the single string. You can also loop all the single crimped ends onto wire and into a bell cap or cone.

Braiding the ends

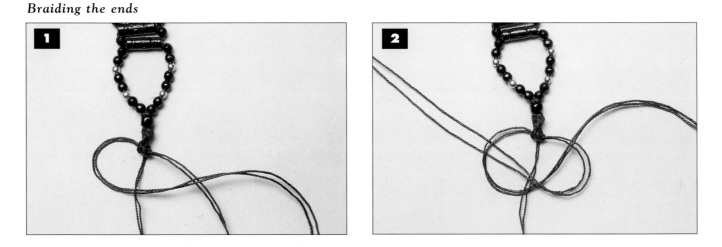

beadwork

The other techniques that we have not discussed are the actual beadwork techniques. Beadwork is usually done with rocailles or bugles, or other small beads, and takes the form of either free-hand weaving, such as the Peyote stitch that we have used on the hat band, or loomwork, such as that used for the evening bag.

Freehand weaving does not have to be done with tiny beads, as we have shown in the Inca choker. To work your beads together as in the example here, use two threads and two needles, and put the threads in from each side of the long beads, so that they cross in the middle, bring the needles back out of the beads, thread a bead or several beads between them, and then thread into the next bead from each side. Keep working in this way. You can also make *fringing* for necklaces, or to go on scarves, by working your threaded needle down through your beads, adding a

Free-hand weaving

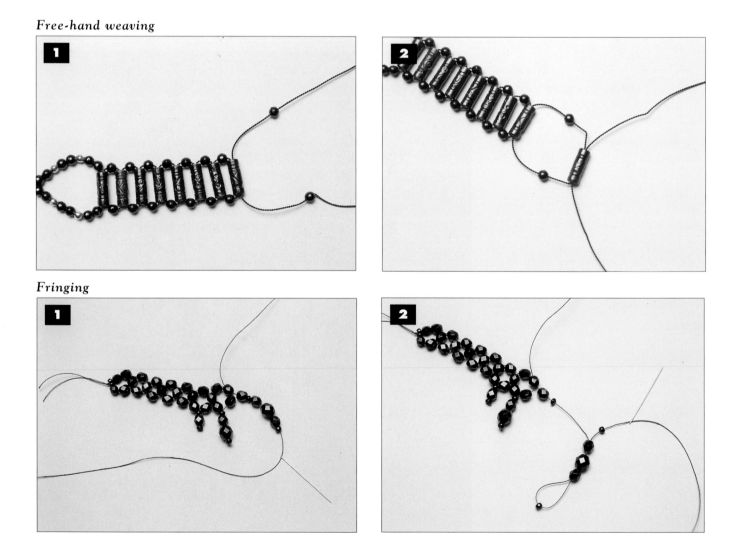

Fringing

small bead at the bottom, and then working back up your other beads. They will hang down and the small bead will hold them in place.

To work in *Peyote stitch*, thread on a few beads (we have used three here), then holding the bottom thread, add another bead and work back into the first bead using the same color and pull your thread through. Then pick up another bead in the same color as the second bead and work back into the second bead, and continue in this way, tightening the thread and making a rope of beads.

Peyote stitch

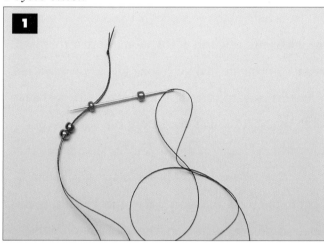

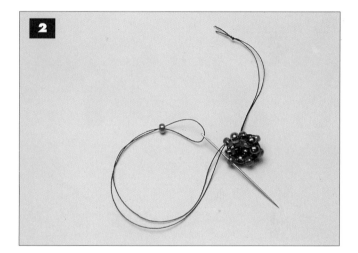

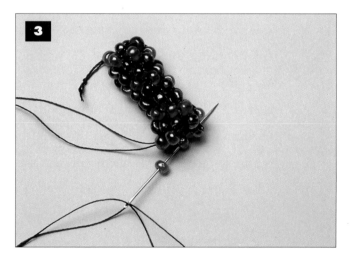

There are many other designs that you can make using freehand weaving; we have only illustrated the ones that are used in the book.

Loomwork is another area that is covered only in its simple forms in the book, though we hope to inspire you to want to learn more. To thread a loom, cut your threads about 10 in (25 cm) longer [at each end] than your work will be and cut one more thread than you will have beads. These are the warp threads. Knot them together and place the knot over the pin on the far end of your loom. Wind them around once or twice so that they are held securely. Now bring the threads back

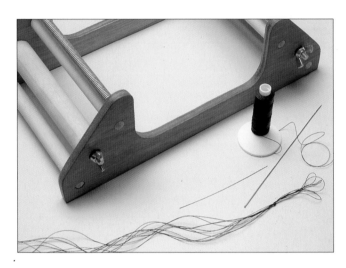

toward you, separating them into the grooves on the loom (it is helpful to use a needle to do this). Tie the loose ends onto this end of the loom, so that they are very taut. If you are making a long piece of work, wind the lengths of warp threads around the roller at the far end, so that it is firmly held, before you tighten your wing nuts, and knot on the loose ends at your end.

To work the beads on the loom, attach your thread to one side, and work a few rows by putting this thread in and out of the warp threads. Then put the beads that you need onto your needle, holding them beneath the warp threads. Bring the beads up between the threads and pull the thread through, then bring your needle back into the same beads, this time making sure that the beading thread goes above the warp threads. Pull the needle tight at the end of each row so that the beads are held firmly. You will continue to work in this way as you add the pattern to your design. It is sensible to work out the design that you are going to use on graph paper before you start. Before you take your work off the loom, work a few rows with just the thread, as you did at the beginning. Work all the loose ends and the warp threads back into your strip of beading.

Loomwork

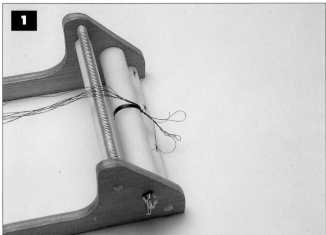

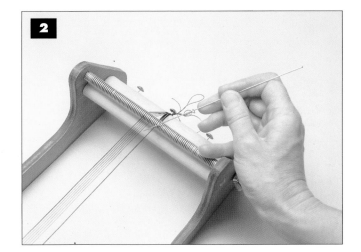

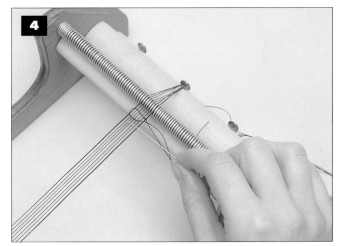

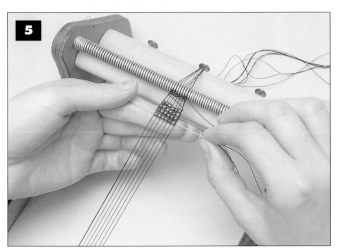

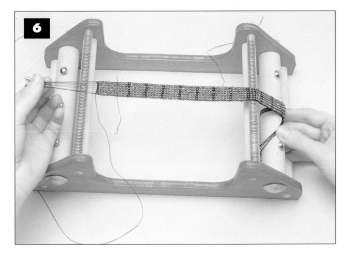

classic

designs

~

triple pearl choker
and earrings

For the necklace:
91 x 10 mm pearls
100 x 0/7 black rocailles
6 french crimps
6 x 3 mm silver-plated
balls
140 cm (4ft 8in) tiger tail
clasp

For the earrings:
2 pearl cabochon
1 pair studs + butterflies

necklace pliers
glue

T his necklace is simple to make but looks very sophisticated. It is worth buying a really beautiful clasp to set off the pearl beads and make the most of them.

1 Thread the pearl beads onto 3 graduated lengths of the tiger tail, with a black rocaille between each bead. We have 28 pearl beads on the top row, 30 on the middle row, and 33 on the bottom row.

2 Finish each row with a rocaille, a silver-plated ball, and another rocaille, and then crimp to the fastener and trim the ends of the tiger tail.

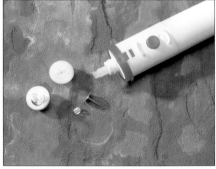

3 For the earrings, simply glue a stud to the back of the cabochon.

black "jet"
choker

YOU WILL NEED:

75 x 8 mm "jet" beads
60 x 6 mm "jet" beads
4 x 5 mm "jet" beads
32 x 0/7 black rocailles
2 calottes
polyester thread
chain
hook

TOOLS:

necklace pliers
fine needles

*T*hese faceted glass beads have been designed to look like jet beads, so we have designed a choker that could have come from a Jane Austin novel. It is made with simple freehand weaving.

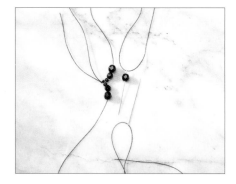

1 & 2 Cut 2 x 5 ft (150 cm) of thread; this is a generous amount, but will save the risk of running out of thread. Use two needles with it. Knot the ends of the threads together. Put a rocaille, a 5 mm bead, and a 6 mm bead onto each thread, then thread into another 6 mm bead from each side so that the threads cross inside the bead. Add another 6 mm bead onto each thread and then again work from each side into the next bead. This is the basic weaving for the choker.

3 After five central beads, put a rocaille, a 6 mm bead, and another rocaille onto your bottom thread. Thread back up through the 6 mm bead and the top rocaille, leaving the bottom one to hold the hanging beads.

4 Continue to weave, adding more hanging beads, and starting to use the larger (8 mm) beads. Return to the smaller beads toward the other end of the choker, so that both ends match.

5 At the end of the choker, make sure that the threads are pulled securely through, so that there are no gaps in the weaving, then knot the ends together. Put a calotte over the knots at both ends.

6 Cut a small piece of chain for each end and open a link in the chain to attach it to the calotte. Add your hook to one side (this can be put into the chain at different lengths so that you can wear the choker in different ways).

knotted Chinese necklace
and earrings

*T*hese lovely Chinese porcelain beads have been combined with little
enameled bead caps to highlight their colors. We have used a thick thread
and knotted between the beads, so that you can learn how to knot while you
make a beautiful necklace.

1 Knot your thread and put a calotte over the knot.

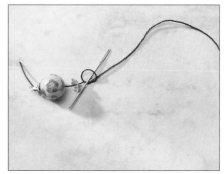

2 Thread the first bead with the bead tips on each side of it and make a knot after the bead (the knot is shown in the techniques section).

3 Continue to add the beads and bead tips and the knot between each bead. Finish with a knot after the last bead. Put another calotte on the knot.

4 Attach the fastener to your calottes.

5 The earrings are simply threaded onto the eyepins with a rolled top.

pearl chain
and earrings

For the chain:
ready-made pearl chain
with 80 beads
10 x 8 mm pearl beads
4 x 6 mm pearl beads
4 x pearl oval beads
14 x 6 mm metallized
plastic rose beads
8 x 3 mm silver-plated
balls
10 x 50 mm eyepins
2 x 25 mm eyepins

For the earrings:
20 x 8 mm pearl beads
32 x 3 mm silver-plated
balls
8 x 0/7 white rocailles
5 cm (2 in) chain
18 x 25 mm (1 in) headpins
2 x 38 mm (1½ in) eyepins
1 pair earwires

round-nose pliers
wirecutters

T*his is a simple way to use ready-made pearl chain with an effective result. We have added very dramatic earrings to go with the simplicity of the chain.*

1 Cut the pearl chain into eight lengths, each of which has 10 of the little pearls on it. Thread the patterns for the straight pieces onto your 50 mm eyepins and roll the tops. We have made four the same and two with different patterns.

2 Gently open the loops on the eyepins to hook in the pieces of chain.

4 For the earrings, start by making the pieces on the headpins, which have a silver-plated ball on the end, a pearl, and then either a white rocaille or another silver-plated ball. Roll the tops of the headpins.

5 Cut two 1 in (2.5 cm) pieces of chain and hook the headpin pieces into them.

3 For the middle and the back of the chain, make linked pearl pieces. Two longer straight pieces are linked onto a short 1 in (25 mm) eyepin which has one pearl on it.

6 Hang the chains from the bottom of the eyepins, put more pearl beads and silver-plated balls onto them, clip the ends, and roll their tops. Attach the earwires to the top of these eyepins.

looped loom
choker

YOU WILL NEED:

1 g 0/8 purple rocailles

110 x 0/7 gray rocailles

3 x 5 mm purple glass
beads

thin black polyester
thread

thick black polyester
thread

TOOLS ETC:

bead loom
fine beading needle
scissors
masking tape
(optional)

T*his choker is dark and sophisticated, but is an easy way to start using a bead loom.*

1 Cut nine 2 ft 6 in (80 cm) lengths of the thin polyester thread and position them on the loom. Both outside edges should have two threads in one groove of the loom to give a firmer edge. Attach another long thin thread to one of the outside warp threads, and work this in and out of alternate warp threads to give a neat beginning to the weaving.

2 Start to work the beads onto the loom. Pick up six beads with your needle and hold them beneath the warp threads, making sure that they fit neatly between each one. Pull the needle and thread through the beads, still holding the beads in place with your finger.

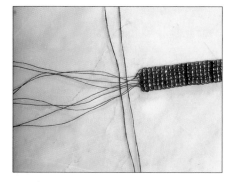

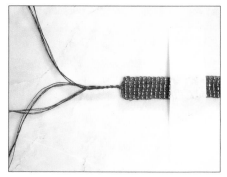

4 Cut two pieces of the thick thread 2 ft (60 cm) long for each end of the choker.

5 Braid on the new threads, using them together, and all the warp threads together. It helps to tape the choker to your work surface so that you can make the braiding firm and close to the end of the weaving.

3 Thread your needle back through the same row of beads, making sure that your needle is above each of the warp threads. Continue weaving, changing to gray beads initially after 10 rows and then after every five rows. Roll the beadwork back toward you as you work along the loom, keeping the work tightly together. You will need to make the choker about 9 in (23 cm) long. Finish with only a few rows of thread as at the beginning, and remove the choker from the loom.

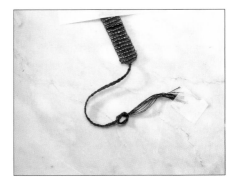

6 When your braiding is long enough to tie the choker around your neck, knot all the ends together and trim them neatly.

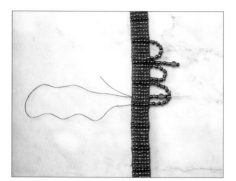

7 If you have loose ends from joining in new threads, work these back into the choker with your needle.

8 Now start on your loop design. Cut a new piece of thin thread and work it through a few rows of work before the third stripe in the choker. Now thread down the stripe, thread on 12 more rocailles, alternating gray and purple, and bring the needle up five rows along, before the next stripe. Work back down this stripe and thread on eight more rocailles in alternate colors and then a purple glass bead. Add one more gray rocaille as "stopper" and thread back up through the glass bead and the rocailles.

9 Work one more loop using 15 rocailles, and then make one using 19 rocailles, both with alternating colors. Your needle should now be threading up through the sixth stripe in your choker. Bring the needle neatly BACK along the top of three rows of looming, working in and out of the outside loom thread, and then thread down the middle row of rocailles. Thread another hanging piece to go into the middle of the loop, using 4 rocailles and another purple glass bead, held with another rocaille. Work back up this to the bottom of the choker, and take the thread back along the bottom of the choker to start to form another of the loops. You can then complete the loop pattern to match the first half, and weave the end of the thread through a few extra rows of rocailles to secure the loops. Finish by trimming any loose ends.

tiffany-style necklace
and earrings

For the necklace:
1 oval porcelain bead
4 tube shape porcelain beads
8 x 8 mm pink glass beads
8 x 6 mm clear glass beads
4 large clear glass drops
2 small clear glass drops
¼ oz (20 g) 0/9 clear rocailles
10 ft (3 m) white polyester thread

For the earrings:
2 oval porcelain beads
6 clear rocailles
2 x 8 mm pink beads
2 x 2 in (50 mm) eyepins
1 pair earwires

scissors
needle
glue
round-nose pliers for the earrings

*P*ale and delicate *with lovely porcelain beads and shimmering glass, this necklace is made to wear long, with an exciting cluster of beads at waist length. There are simple earrings to compliment it.*

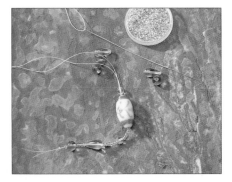

1 Cut 8 ft (2.5 m) of thread and use it doubled in a needle. Knot the ends and put glue onto the knot. When the glue is dry, thread the first beads, drops, and rocailles onto the thread and then the large oval bead.

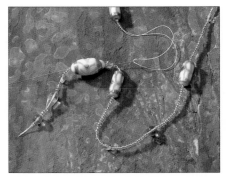

2 Thread on, working the round beads, tubes, and drops into the rocailles and making a long plain area for the back of the necklace. Keep working back down the necklace, while checking that the two sides match. Now thread back into the round bead, rocaille, and oval porcelain bead near the beginning of the necklace. Put on the last few beads and knot at the end. Put a drop of glue onto the knot.

3 Cut another 1 ft 8 in (50 cm) length of thread, and use it doubled in a needle again. Knot and glue the end and thread a few more of the hanging beads. Carefully knot this thread under the oval bead and above the hanging pieces.

4 Thread on the last few beads and knot the end of this thread. Trim off the loose ends.

5 The earrings are simply made by putting the beads onto the eyepins with a rolled top.

evening
bag

YOU WILL NEED:

3 oz (90 g) 0/7 iridescent blue rocailles
¾ oz (20 g) 0/7 iridescent clear rocailles
⅜ oz (10 g) 0/7 light blue rocailles
a piece of black felt 4 x 8 in *(10 x 20 cm)*
5 ft (1.5 m) black cord

TOOLS ETC:

bead loom
beading needle
scissors
glue
needle

This project will require time and patience, but your effort will be rewarded. The bag is made in strips on a bead loom, then lined with felt, and finished with cords. It is big enough to carry your keys and some money for a glamorous night out.

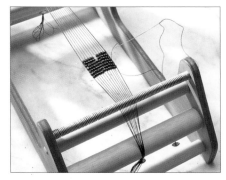

1 Set up the bead loom as shown in the techniques section. There are 11 rocailles in each strip. You will need three strips, and there are 57 rows in each strip. Remember to introduce the color changes differently on the central strip.

2 When the three strips are complete, work the loose threads at the sides of the strips back into the weaving. Then connect the strips together by running a thread through all of the pieces.

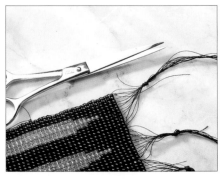

3 Knot the warp threads together and trim them.

4 Glue the piece of felt to the beading, making sure that all the loose ends of threads are trapped between the two.

5 Sew neatly along all the edges so that the felt and the beading cannot separate.

6 Fold the piece in half and sew the cord down the sides, making sure that you have the bottom of the cord neatly tucked under.

amber necklace
and earrings

*B*eautiful chunks of Baltic amber are threaded with plain chunky silver beads and ornate bead tips as a centerpiece. The amber is so lovely that it does not need to have much added to it.

1 Join the silk thread to the fastener with knots (as shown in the techniques section). Five knots were used here.

2 Thread the beads onto the silk, using the bead tips on the central bead.

3 Join the split ring to the necklace using five knots as before.

4 The earrings are simply put onto the eyepins and the tops are rolled. The earwires are put into the top loop on the eyepins.

AQM

ethnic
designs
~

pipe
choker

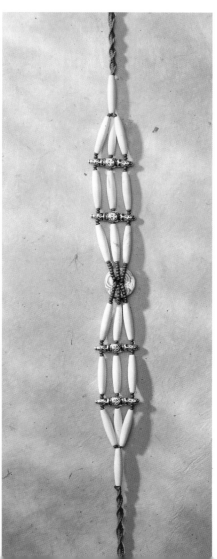

1 ceramic ring
20 pipe beads
140 x 0/7 brown rocailles
4 spacer bars
12 ft (360 cm) of waxed
thread
10½ ft (280 cm) brown
cord

TOOLS ETC:

scissors
glue
tape (optional)

This is a nice easy way to use pipe beads and create a dramatic effect with them. The pipe beads are actually plastic, but they look very natural. We have put them together with some elaborate spacer bars and a pretty ceramic ring to create a piece that is light and easy to wear.

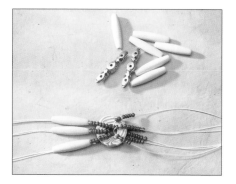

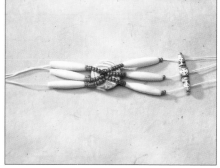

1 Cut 6 x 2 ft (60 cm) lengths of the waxed thread, and thread 16 rocailles onto each one. Thread three onto each side of the ceramic ring, and arrange the rocailles so that they are evenly positioned on the threads inside the ring.

2 Work on into the second spacer bar and more pipe beads, and then work all the threads into a single pipe bead. Repeat on the other side of the ring. Move all the beads back up the threads so that there are no gaps.

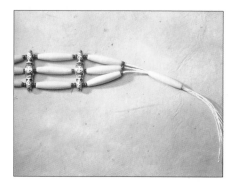

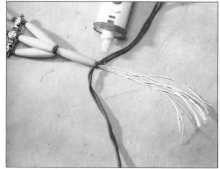

3 Now thread both ends of each thread through a pipe bead, so that you have three on each side, add the rocailles, and work the double thread into a spacer bar.

4 Cut two 4½ ft (140 cm) lengths of the brown cord and tie one around each bunch of waxed threads. When you have tied the cords to the threads, add a drop of glue so that they will not slide down the waxed threads.

5 Braid each cord around the waxed threads, as shown in the techniques section. You may find it easier to tape the choker to your work top while you braid. Knot the ends of your braiding threads at the bottom of the waxed threads and leave trailing pieces of the brown cord.

cinnabar
cluster

*A*pple coral and cinnabar beads in three strong strands are held by a dramatic centerpiece.

1 Cut three lengths of thread about 2 ft (60 cm) long, lay them out, and start to plan your design. You will be using nearly all of the beads on the main strands. Keep 3 x 10 mm apple coral beads, 15 x 5 mm black beads, 19 brown tile beads, 3 sandalwood beads, and 40 black rocailles to make the centerpiece with the large cinnabar bead, and the ends of the necklace. In this design you will need to keep the center of the strands quite plain, use smaller beads at the ends of the strands, and space your larger beads evenly through the design. Your strands should be very slightly different lengths and should hang well together.

2 Finish each end of the strands by making a neat loop with french crimps. Trim off any loose ends of thread. Cut the wire into two pieces and make a generous loop at one end of the pieces. This is opened sideways so that the ends of the necklace strands can be hung from it, and then closed again. Thread a cone onto each of the wires so that the ends of the strands are neatly covered. Add a few more beads to these wires on each side. Then roll the wires and use this loop to attach your fastener.

3 Make the centerpiece by cutting a 1 ft (30 cm) piece of thread and knotting one end. Put a drop of glue onto the knot and allow it to dry. Thread up into the large cinnabar bead, put on more of the smaller beads, and then thread back into the large bead.

4 Finish with the last few beads and make another knot in your thread. Use a needle to draw the knot close to the bottom of the beads, and put a little glue onto this end. Trim the thread close to the knots. You can now loop the centerpiece around the middle of the necklace

peruvian
string

S imple but stylish – with a few tricks to make your necklace look really professional.

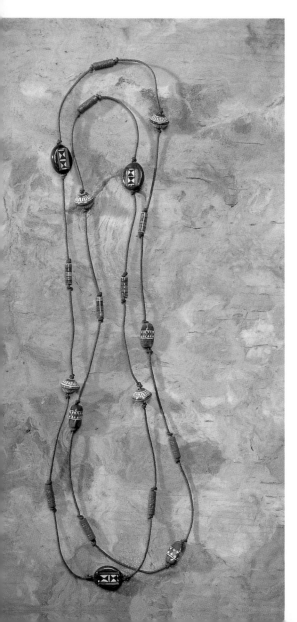

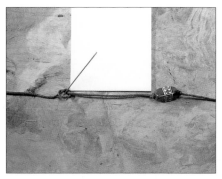

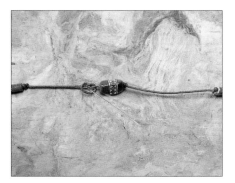

1 Cut a 6 ft (180 cm) length of the blue linen thread and position a bead in the middle of it. Make a knot on each side of the bead and use a needle to move the knots close to the central bead. Use a measuring block to make the spaces between your beads. (Ours is roughly 2 inches long). Position the block next to the knot that you have just made, and use a needle to move another knot into position at the end of the block.

2 You can now thread on another bead, and knot close to the other side of this bead. Continue with your beads, knots, and spaces, working on both sides of the string, moving away from your central bead.

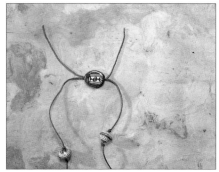

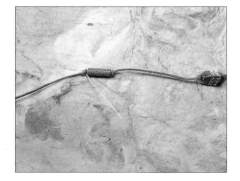

3 Thread both ends of the string through each side of your last bead.

4 Use your measuring block to check the distance between this bead and the ones on each side of it, and make a knot on both sides of the last bead. Put a drop of glue onto these knots and trim the ends of the string very neatly.

lapis lazuli and
turquoise necklace

1 x 3 ft (90 cm) string of
Chinese turquoise chips
1 large lapis lazuli bead
4 x 8 mm lapis lazuli beads
4 coral chunks
14 x 7 mm Thai silver
beads
3 cards of no. 5 black silk
thread
2 calottes
Balinese hook fastener +
jump ring

necklace pliers
scissors
fishing line (to plan
the necklace on)

This necklace is a wonderful combination of chips of Chinese turquoise, large lapis lazuli beads from Afghanistan, old coral from Nepal, and tiny silver beads from Thailand. It is completed with a Balinese clasp. A necklace for dreaming of faraway places!

1 & **2** The chips of turquoise cannot be counted to get even lengths, and the odd sizes need to be balanced around the necklace, so it makes sense with this

necklace to plan it on fishing line. You can also reject any damaged chips or ones that sit badly at this stage.

3 Unwind the silk thread on your cards and knot the ends together. Put some glue onto the knot and then put a calotte over the knot. Rethread your necklace onto the silk, working each section back toward the calotte as you thread.

4 Finish with another knot and calotte as before. Attach the hook and the jump ring to the calottes.

Indian braided
beads

YOU WILL NEED:

10 assorted Indian metal beads

4 skeins of embroidery floss in different colors

TOOLS ETC:

scissors

small piece of tiger tail

tape (optional)

This is an effective way to use a few special beads, and makes an interesting change from putting them on leather. Use really bright threads that pick up the colors of the beads and make them look bright and beautiful.

1 Cut 16½ ft (5 m) of each color thread, which you will use doubled. Then cut two 3¼ ft (1 m) lengths of two of the colors, which will go through the middle of the beads as the core threads. Thread one of the beads onto the middle of these two pieces.

2 Knot the braiding threads onto the core threads. Start to braid over the core threads, as shown in the techniques section. You may find tape useful to hold the braid in place.

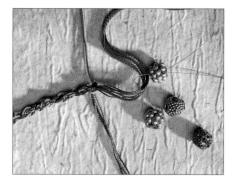

3 When you have made 4½ in (11 cm) of braiding, put a bead onto the core threads. You may need to double the piece of tiger tail around the core threads to work them through the bead.

4 Bring your braiding threads around the sides of the bead, and start to braid again on the other side.

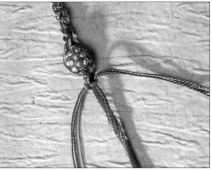

5 Braid the threads 10 times between the beads. Continue to add the other eight beads.

6 When you have added all the beads, braid for another 3½ in (9 cm) and knot the threads together. Using the core threads and the braiding threads, make two tiny braids, just long enough to go over a bead. Then knot all the threads together again and trim the ends so that they are all the same length.

Inca choker
and earrings

For the choker:

1 x 1 in (25 mm) metallized plastic Inca disk

16 Peruvian ceramic tubes

2 x 5 mm black glass beads

60 x 4 mm round black beads

12 x 3 mm gold-plated balls

2 cards no. 5 black silk thread

13 ft (4 m) thick black thread

For the earrings:

2 x ¾ in (18 mm) Inca discs

2 x 2 in (50 mm) gold-plated eyepins

4 x 3 mm gold-plated balls

8 x 4 mm black beads

1 pair gold-plated or gold earwires

round-nose pliers for earrings
scissors
tape (optional)

Small ceramic tube beads have been woven together on each side of a metallized plastic "Inca" disk. Then it is tied around the neck so that you can wear it as tight as you like. It will not take long to make, and you might find yourself wearing it every day. We have used black beads, but you could let your imagination run riot and have a rainbow of colors around your neck.

1 Unwind the silk on the cards, and knot the threads together about 7 in (18 cm) from the end. Thread on the first few beads and balls.

2 Thread into the first tube from each side, so that the threads cross inside it.

3 Add another 4 mm bead onto each of the threads before you thread into the next tube. Continue to weave in and out of the tubes until you have eight tubes on this side.

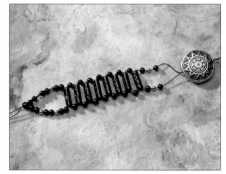

4 Thread the central beads and balls onto each thread and then bring both of them through the Inca disk.

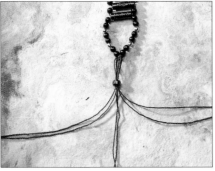

5 Repeat the weaving through the tubes on the other side of the Inca disk. Tighten the beads and tubes on the threads and then knot them together. Cut a 6½ ft (2 m) length of thick black thread for each end, fold each in half, and attach them to the ends of the choker by the knots. Slip a 5 mm black bead on at each end, and braid the ends below these beads. Knot the end of the braiding and trim the ends.

Thread the earrings onto the eyepins with a rolled top.

native American
belt

A *very bright, cheerful representation of a Native American beaded belt. The one that we show here has patterns that we have designed, rather than authentic ones. If you wanted to make your belt more traditional, you could check original colors and designs in a library, and make yourself a more true representation.*

1 Thread your loom as shown in the techniques section, and start to work on your rocailles. There are 11 rocailles across the belt.

2 Follow the pattern, or design your own pattern and complete that. This beaded strip is 2 ft 1 in (64 cm) long. When you have taken it off the loom, work all the loose threads back into the work. Tie your warp threads together so that they can be hidden away.

3 Cut the two pieces of chamois. We have cut them from a piece from an auto supply store. Sew the two strips together, and cut a small patch to go over the seam.

4 Glue the beading to the leather, making sure that the knotted warp threads are carefully tucked beneath the beading and the leather. Then sew the beading to the leather for extra strength. Fringe the ends of the leather.

5 Finally, thread on the beads and knot the fringe beneath the beads.

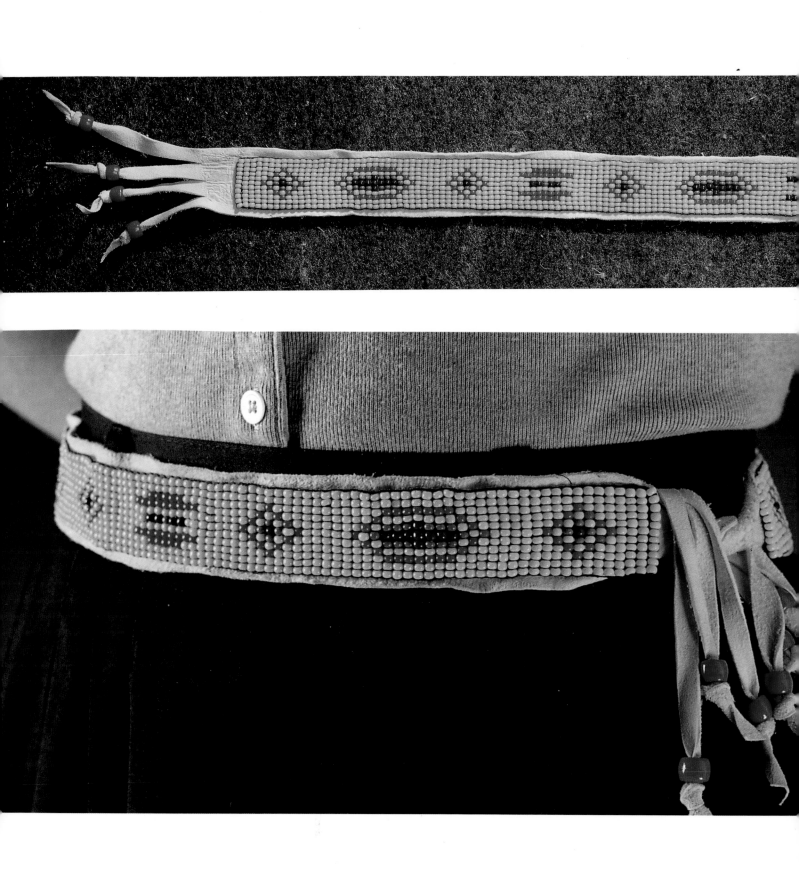

African beads
on leather

a pendant
6 Venetian millefiore
beads
6 Venetian eye beads
26 Ghanaian powder
glass beads
40 old silver rings
18 mm bead with a wide
hole
5 x 5 mm black glass
beads
2 spring ends for leather
3¼ ft (1 m) natural
leather thonging

wire cutters
pliers

These are old Venetian glass beads that were sent to West Africa, and old powder glass beads from Ghana. The pendant piece is made by the Lobi people and shows a coin and snakes; the snakes are considered to have protective powers.

1 Arrange your beads on your leather with a silver ring between each one.

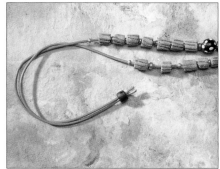

2 Work both ends of the leather through the wide-holed bead. Make sure that it is a strong bead.

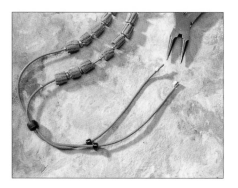

3 Clip the loops off the spring ends and squeeze them onto the ends of the leather with the other small black beads behind them.

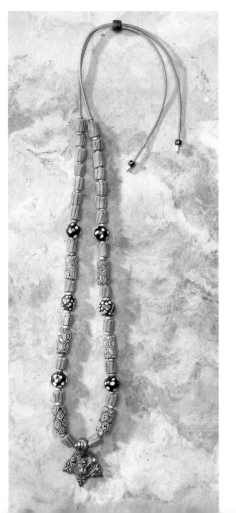

Thai silver necklace
and earrings

A simple but stunning arrangement of silver beads from Thailand. The beads are made using the traditional skills of the Khymer craftsmen, who have come over the borders from Cambodia.

1 Start by knotting your thread onto the fastener (as shown in the techniques section); there are four knots between the first bead and the fastener.

2 Thread your beads. As these beads are handmade, they are slightly different shapes and sizes, and you should arrange them so they sit well together.

3 Finish by knotting onto the jump ring at the other side of the necklace.

4 The earrings are simple straight earrings with rolled tops.

glitz
designs

triangles necklace
and ear-rings

For the necklace:
72 x 8 mm blue faceted beads
107 x 0/7 gray rocailles
8 x blue triangle beads
2 calottes
1 fastener
10 ft (3 m) black polyester thread

For the earrings:
4 blue triangle beads
6 x 0/7 gray rocailles
2 x 8 mm blue faceted beads
4 x 1½ in (38 mm) eyepins
1 pair earwires

necklace pliers
round-nose pliers for the earrings
2 fine needles

A striking combination of iridescent beads and angular shapes all work together to produce a necklace that will allow you to make an entrance – anywhere.

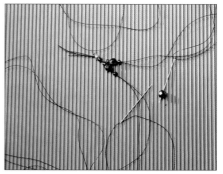

1 Cut two 5 ft (150 cm) lengths of thread and use them doubled on the fine needles. Knot the ends and put a calotte over the knot. Thread a rocaille onto both pairs of threads; separate the threads into the first faceted beads with rocailles on each side of them. Bring all the threads into the next bead, working from both sides so that the threads cross in the center of the bead.

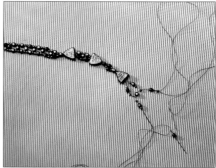

2 Continue to weave through the first section of beads, then bring both threads through a triangle bead. Now use triangles and weaving, changing the direction of the triangle beads as you work.

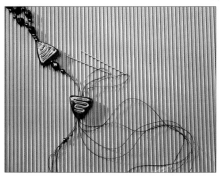

3 Bring both threads through the hanging beads, put a rocaille onto the bottom, and thread back up through the beads above it, so that the rocaille holds the beads on the hanging piece.

4 Repeat your design on the other side of the choker. When you have finished, check that the beads are neatly positioned on the threads, then knot again at this side and put another calotte over the knot. Add the fastener.

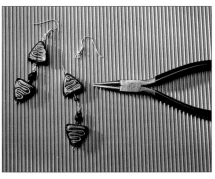

5 The loop on the top of the bottom eyepin on the earrings is linked into the bottom of the top eyepin, so that the earring has extra movement.

baubles and
bangle set

This set is a lovely mixture of bright colors and dull silver-colored beads. We started our design with the clips for the earrings and added the glass rose beads to compliment the fruit and flowers pattern on them. Next came the chic bracelet, again with little roses, and finally a simple twist necklace with the last few glass roses entwined in it.

1 For the necklace cut three 1½ ft (45 cm) lengths of tiger tail and attach them to one end of the fastener with crimps. Thread the beads and crimp again at the other end. The necklace can be worn plain or twisted.

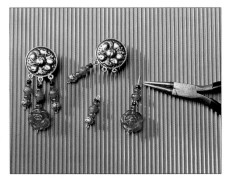

2 To make the earrings, thread the beads onto the eyepins, clip them to length, and roll the tops to attach them to the clips.

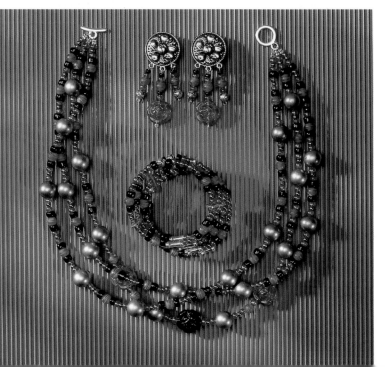

4 Now thread beads onto the top two wires and add a three-hole spacer to these new wires. Join in the top wire from the first pair. Work on around on all of the wires, putting the same pattern into the center.

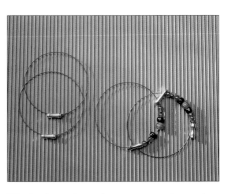

3 The bracelet is the most complicated piece to make. Cut the lengths of wire and glue four safety ends to each of them. Thread the first few beads onto the bottom two wires and thread on a two-hole spacer bar.

5 Reverse the pattern around to the other side, adding the other spacer bars. Then glue the safety ends to the other side to keep all the beads in place.

rope
necklace

1½ oz (40 g) 0/7 white rocailles

¾ oz (20 g) each of 0/7 turquoise, light blue, and dark gray rocailles

1 metallized plastic bead

16½ ft (5 m) fine white polyester thread

4 ft (1.25 m) white waxed thread

ring clasp

fine needle

scissors

glue

This is a very easy necklace to make. Lots of rocaille beads are threaded into long strings and looped together. You could wear them just like that, clasped so that the strings are twisted together. Or you can add a tassel to make them more exciting.

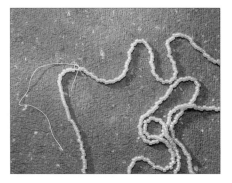

1 Cut the fine thread into 3¼ ft (1 m) lengths and make two strings of white rocailles, and one each of turquoise, light blue, and dark gray. The strings of rocailles should measure 3 ft (90 cm) long, which allows you length to knot the threads. Put a drop of glue onto the knot and trim the ends.

2 These can now be held together with the clasp. Twist them before you wear them.

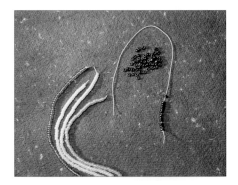

3 Cut five 20 cm (8 in) lengths of the waxed thread for the tassel. Knot the ends of the threads and put a drop of glue onto the knots. When this is dry, thread on the rocailles, again two strands of white and one each of the other colors. Leave enough space to knot the other end of the thread. Do not knot too close to the rocailles, as you do not want the tassel to be rigid. Put another drop of glue onto these knots and trim all ends.

4 Put your last piece of waxed thread into the middle of these strands and thread it into the metallized plastic bead.

5 Thread in pattern onto the other side of the large bead, 14 rocailles on one side, 15 on the other. Knot the two ends of thread firmly together, again put on a drop of glue, and trim the ends. This can just slide over your necklace twist. Matching earrings can be made with shorter tassels, and using an eyepin to come up through the big bead.

Greek tubes and bars
necklace and earrings

For the necklace:
2 x 3-hole spacer bars
40 Greek ceramic tubes
51 x 0/7 metallic purple rocailles
fastener
french crimps
hatpin or stiff wire
tiger tail

For the earrings:
2 ceramic tubes
4 small ceramic square beads
2 x 6 mm metallized plastic balls
10 x 0/7 purple rocailles
2 x 2 in (50 mm) eyepins
1 pair earwires

strong round-nose pliers
necklace pliers
wire cutters
file

T*his necklace is glamorous and stylish – the strength of the beads compliment the strong shape of the design.*

1 Cut either a stiff wire or a hatpin wire to a 5 in (12 cm) length and smooth the ends with a file. Roll one end with your pliers and thread on the rocailles and the tubes and the spacer bars. Then roll the top of the wire.

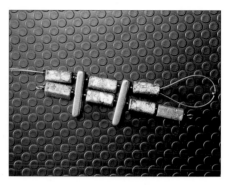

2 Cut two 2½ ft (74 cm) lengths of tiger tail. Fold one in half and put a rocaille into the middle of the length. Now using the tiger tail doubled, thread more tubes and rocailles and work through one side of the spacer bars.

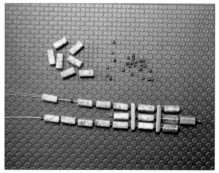

3 Repeat this on the other side of the spacers with the other length of tiger tail and work up both sides of the necklace, alternating tubes and rocailles.

4 Push all the beads back down the tiger tail and make neat loops at the ends with french crimps. Hook the fastener into these loops.

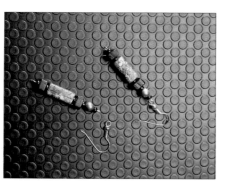

5 Use the 2 in (50 mm) eyepins to make matching earrings. These are simple drop earrings.

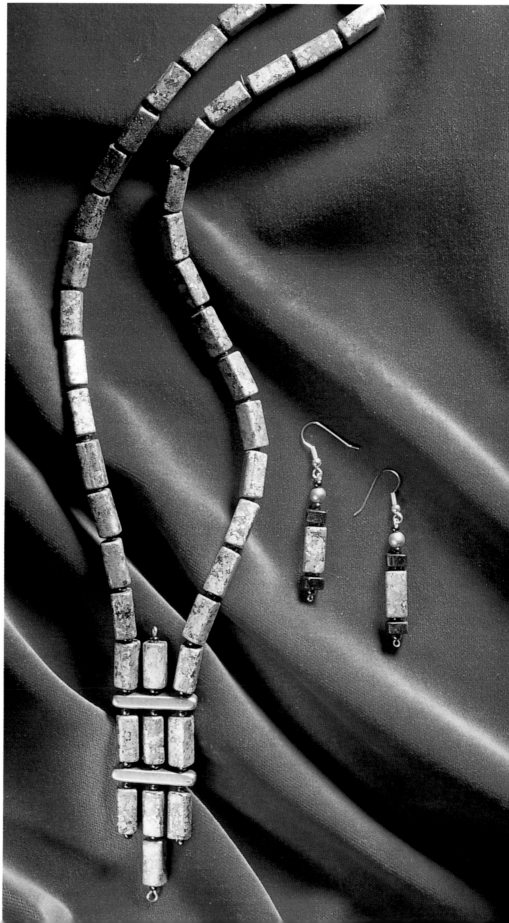

pink glitz necklace
and earrings

A s the name suggests, this is another really glitzy necklace. Both the rocailles and the round beads have a extra sheen and depth to their color to add to the richness of the piece.

YOU WILL NEED:

For the necklace:
26 x 8 mm pink beads
52 x 6 mm pink beads
2 antiqued gold triangles
1 antiqued gold ring
4 ft 8 in (140 cm) black thread
10 gilt french crimps
22 x 3 mm gold-plated balls
180 x 0/6 red rocailles
1 ornate fastener

For the earrings:
6 x 1½ in (38 mm) eyepins
22 x 0/6 red rocailles
14 x 3 mm gold-plated balls
8 x 8 mm pink beads
6 x 6 mm pink beads
2 x antiqued gold triangles.
1 pair earwires

TOOLS ETC:

*round-nose pliers for the earrings
necklace pliers
scissors*

1 Cut three pieces of the thread, increasing in length between 1 ft and 1 ft 2 in (30 and 35 cm). Thread the ring into the middle of them and then arrange the pink beads and rocailles onto each of the threads.

2 When you have finished the arrangement, crimp the ends of the threads onto the triangles, putting a rocaille between the crimp and the triangle.

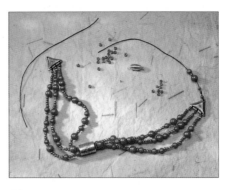

3 Cut two 6 in (15 cm) lengths of thread and crimp these to the tops of the triangles in the same arrangement as before, then thread the beads onto these threads. Attach the fastener with crimps, again putting a rocaille between the fastener and the crimps at each end.

4 Make the hanging pieces for the earrings by threading the eyepins and rolling their tops. Then open these loops sideways to hang the pieces from the triangles. Put the earwire into the top of the triangle.

red hearts necklace
and earrings

For the necklace:
5 metallized plastic hearts
4 red lacquered hearts
12 x 8 mm red hearts
20 x 8 mm a.b. hearts
24 x 5 mm red hearts
12 x 6 mm round a.b beads
27 x 5 mm black glass beads
130 x 0/7 black rocailles
34 x 0/7 red rocailles
2 french crimps
56 x 1 in (25 mm) eyepins
1 ft 8 in (50 cm) red thread

For the earrings:
2 metallized plastic hearts
2 x 8 mm a.b. hearts
8 x 0/7 black rocailles
4 x 0/7 red rocailles
2 x 2 in (50 mm) eyepins
1 pair earwires

necklace pliers
round-nose pliers
scissors
wire cutters

This necklace is really glitzy. Lots of different-sized hearts, in different colors, are all threaded together into a Valentine's riot.

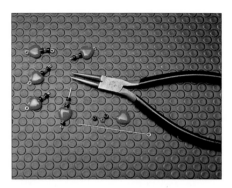

1 Start by making the little eyepin pieces for the necklace, simply threading the beads and rolling the tops of the eyepins. There are: 20 x large a.b. heart + black rocaille; 12 x large red heart + black, red, black rocailles; 16 x small red heart + black, red rocailles; 4 x small red heart + black, red, black rocailles; 2 x small red heart + black rocaille. The eyepins should be clipped to the appropriate length before you roll them, as shown in the techniques section.

2 Start to thread your necklace from the center. Put on one rocaille and then thread both ends into a heart, a rocaille, and a 5 mm black bead before you separate the threads and add the red lacquered hearts.

3 Thread the eyepin pieces on with the beads in small clusters. There are nine in each of the first two clusters, and five in the second two. Between them, thread the large hearts and the black glass beads, with black rocailles beside them.

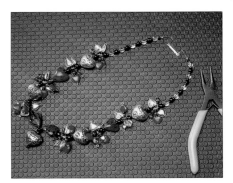

4 When you have threaded the main part of the necklace, work to the end with the plainer beads, and crimp on the fastener.

5 The earrings are simply threaded onto the eyepins with a rolled top.

gilt chain
and earrings

This chain is very simple to make. We have seen a very similar one for sale in a store in Los Angeles for nearly $100; think of that as you make your own!

YOU WILL NEED:

For the chain:
2 ft 4 in (70 cm) chain
10 x 2 in (50 mm) eyepins
34 x 3 mm gold-plated balls
14 x 0/8 purple rocailles
8 x 0/8 green rocailles
6 x 5 mm crystal lice-shaped beads
8 x 4 mm crystal diamonds
4 x 6 mm metallized plastic gold-plated roses
10 x 8 mm metallized plastic gold-plated roses
1 crystal drop
20 x gold-plated daisy lice
1 x 6 mm jump ring

For the earrings:
8 x 1½ in (38 mm) eyepins
4 x 1 in (25 mm) eyepins
4 in (10 cm) chain
10 x 5 mm crystal diamonds
40 x 3 mm gold-plated balls
6 x 0/8 purple rocailles
2 x 6 mm jump rings
1 pair earwires

TOOLS ETC:

round-nose pliers
wire cutters

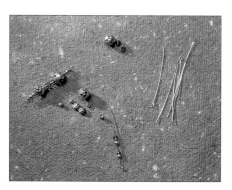

1 Make your straight pieces by threading the beads onto the eyepins and rolling the tops as shown in the techniques section.

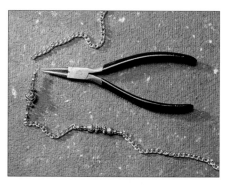

2 Cut eight pieces of chain that are 2 in (5 cm) long, and one piece that is 1 ft (30 cm). Gently open the loops at the top and bottom of your eyepins sideways, and slip in the lengths of chain, to make up the pattern.

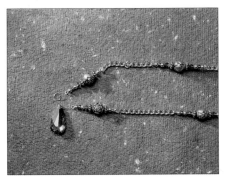

3 Finish with a straight piece at each end, and join these with a jump ring through their loops and through the crystal drop.

4 For the earrings, make the hanging pieces on the eyepins first, clipping them to length where necessary. Thread these onto the last 1½ in (38 mm) eyepins, and roll the ends of these, making sure that the new loops face in the same direction as the ready-made loops.

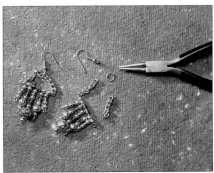

5 Gently open the loops sideways, and add the pieces of chain [four 1 in (2.5 cm) lengths]. At the top of the earrings use the jump rings to join the chain, and to attach the earwires.

night sky
necklace

M ultistrands of stars, moons, and birds, and a dramatic hematite donut, all hang from tiny dark iridescent rocailles.

YOU WILL NEED:

1 hematite donut
(¾ in (20 mm))

1 sun

6 round mosque beads

12 cube mosque beads

10 mother-of-pearl birds

84 x 5 or 6 mm glass beads
in black, purple, and
blues

2 tiny heart beads

6 black ceramic birds

15 iridescent miracle
beads (6 – 8 mm)

6 stars

2 moons

a few 3 mm silver-plated
balls

c 350 x 0/7 dark
iridescent rocailles

2 cones

fastener

tiger tail

french crimps

0.8 silver wire

9 figure-8 fittings

black polyester thread

TOOLS ETC:

necklace pliers
wire cutters
scissors
round-nose pliers

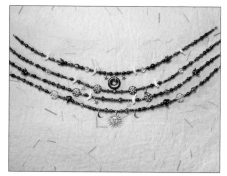

1 Cut a 2½ in (6 cm) piece of wire, put it through the donut, and cross the ends over. Form one end into a neat loop with your pliers. Use your fingers to wrap the other wire around the bottom of this loop. When you have covered the bottom of the loop with a few neat coils, clip off any extra wire and press the end of the wire into the loop above the coils with your pliers. The figure-8 fittings are used to hang the sun, and the tiny stars and moons.

2 Cut four 1 ft 8 in (50 cm) lengths of thread and start to thread on the beads. The donut and the sun should be in the same position on the threads. Space all the bigger beads and the hanging pieces in the more central part of the strands, and work toward plainer, smaller beads at the sides. You need to keep a selection of beads to go on each side of the cones. When you feel that your threading is right, hold the strands up to see how they hang. If you want them all to hang together, the strand with the donut should be the shortest.

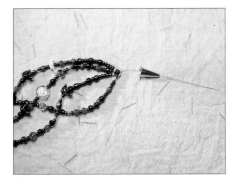

3 Finish all the ends by making neat loops with the french crimps, then trim any loose ends. Cut a 5 in (12 cm) length of tiger tail for each end and make a loop at one end with crimps. Thread the tiger tail through the ends of the necklace strands and back into its own loop. Thread a cone over the ends of the necklace strands.

4 Your last few beads are then threaded onto the tiger tail, and you can attach the fastener at the ends with more french crimps. Finally, trim any loose ends.

modern art choker
and earrings

For the choker:
1 wooden square bead
1 blue circle bead
1 pink triangle bead
1 pink small square bead
1 mauve small square bead
2 small blue cubes
2 green cubes
2 yellow lice beads
2 red washer beads
2 pink round beads
4 x 0/7 black rocailles
1½ ft (45 cm) round black tubing
1 packet of 0.8 jewelry wire
1½ in (4 cm) 1.2 jewelry wire

For the earrings:
2 mauve small square beads
2 pink triangle beads
2 red washer beads
2 yellow lice beads
2 large green cubes
2 small blue cubes
2 pink round beads
8 x 0/7 black rocailles
2 x 2 in (50 mm) eyepins
2 x 1 in (25 mm) eyepins
1 pair earwires

round-nose pliers
wire cutters
flat-nose pliers

*N*ot all projects with beads need to have lots of threading. With this necklace we have wired most of the beads so that they hang flat, and threaded a few, to create a bright, primary choker.

1 Start by wiring the beads that are going to hang flat, as shown in the techniques section. Check that the loop you make is large enough for the rubber tubing to go through, before you make the coils at the bottom of it. Cut about 3 in (8 cm) of wire for each bead.

2 Cut another two pieces of wire the same length, make a neat loop at the bottom, and thread on the beads to make the hanging pieces. Make a large loop above the beads so that it will go over the rubber tubing and coil your wire below it.

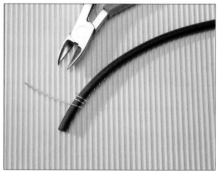

3 Use the end of the rubber tubing to make the spirals that go around it.

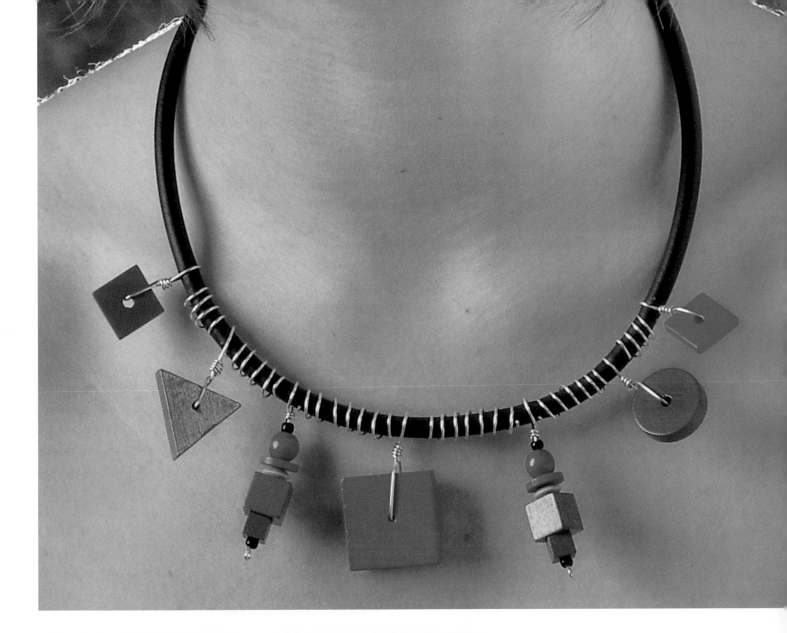

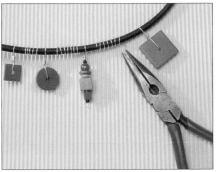

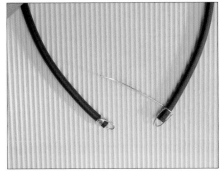

4 Thread the design onto the tubing and gently press the ends of the spirals into the rubber so that the pattern remains separated. You can gently press in the loops above the beads as well, so that they stay in place.

5 Make another loop at the end of the rubber tubing, turn the wire at an angle to it, and wind the wire around the loose end. Attach a hook to this and hook it into the other side to fasten the choker.

Make the earrings by linking the two eyepins together when you have threaded the beads.

glass fantasy necklace
and earrings

For the necklace:
9 assorted glass nuggets
37 blue drops
51 blue and green teardrops
52 x 6 mm blue and green round glass beads
18 x 0/8 rocailles in green or blue
60 x 3 mm silver-plated balls
2 cones
4 x 1½ in (38 mm) eyepins
10 crimps
5½ ft (170 cm) blue thread
1 card 0.8 silver-plated wire

For the earrings:
2 matching nuggets
1 pair earstuds + friction nuts

round-nose pliers
necklace pliers
wire cutters
glue for earrings

T*his is a lovely, over-the-top combination of beads, wire, and glass nuggets. The nuggets are usually sold for display or flower arranging, but they combine beautifully with the rich blues and greens of the beads to make a really exotic necklace.*

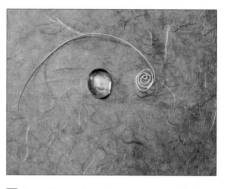

1 Start by working the wire around the glass nuggets. Cut a 10 in (25 cm) length of wire and make a coil at the beginning of it. Press a glass bauble into the coil so that it starts to enclose it.

2 Continue to wrap the wire around the nugget until it is held firmly in place.

3 Make a loop above the nugget and coil the wire around the bottom of the loop, as shown in the techniques section. Trim off any excess wire. Wire the other nuggets in the same way.

4 Put four of the glass drops onto eyepins, roll the top to hang with the beads. Now plan the design for the necklace on your threads. Cut three 1 ft 4 in (40 cm) lengths of thread, and work your beads, nuggets, and drops onto the threads. Arrange them so that the colors and shapes are well balanced, and finish each of the threads with the rocailles which will go inside the cones.

 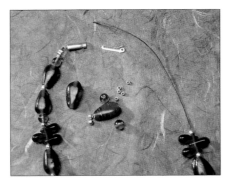

5 When you are happy with these threads, crimp a neat loop at their ends. Cut two 6 in (15 cm) lengths of threads and make a loop with crimps at one end. Thread these through the loops at the ends of the main threads, and back into themselves. Then put the cones over the ends.

6 Thread the rest of the beads above the cones and finish by crimping on the fastener.

7 The studs are glued onto the back of the two nuggets to make matching earrings.

chain
belt

YOU WILL NEED:

12 ceramic disk beads
1 card 1.2 silver-plated
wire
2 ft (60 cm) large link
silver-colored chain
(from a hardware store)
2½ in (6 cm) 0/8 silver-
plated wire (optional)

TOOLS ETC:

strong round-nose
pliers
an extra pair of
strong pliers
wire cutters
file

An idea for something different that you can make with beads. These large disks are from Rajastan in India, and have lovely soft colors, but they are a little heavy for necklaces or earrings.

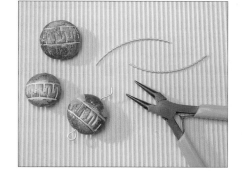

1 Cut lengths of wire to go through your disks [you will need about 2½ in (6 cm) for each bead]. Make a large loop at each side of 11 of the beads. The 12th bead has one large and one small loop.

2 Open the chain in three-link lengths (you may need to use two pairs of pliers to do this), and link the chain and the beads together, ending with the 12th bead with the small loop at the very end.

3 Add two extra links of chain before the first bead. Make a hook with 2½ in (6 cm) of the thicker wire as shown in the techniques section. As an extra decoration, you can wrap the thin wire around the hook if you like.

flowers and leaves necklace
and earrings

8 tiny plastic flowers
8 larger flowers
8 smaller leaves
5 larger leaves
4 white glass drop beads
13 figure-8 findings
16 x 1 in (25 mm) silver-
plated headpins
38 x 6 mm clear beads
76 x 0/7 pearl rocailles
16 x 0/7 clear rocailles
30 x 6 mm clear glass
beads
8 x 8 mm pink glass beads
tiger tail
4 french crimps
fastener

round-nose pliers
necklace pliers
scissors

T*his is a delicate, pretty necklace with pastel leaves and flowers, which is very light and easy to wear in the summer.*

1 Put the leaves onto the figure-8 findings.

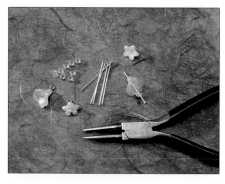

2 Put the headpins into the flowers (with a rocaille inside them) and make a loop on top of them.

3 & **4** Arrange your flowers, leaves, and

beads onto the tiger tail and crimp the fastener on at each end.

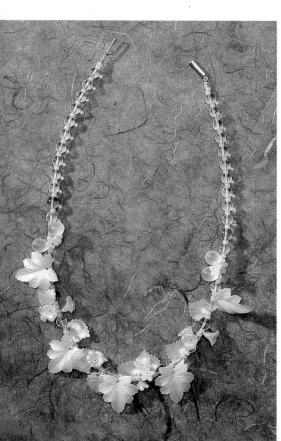

"donuts" necklace
and earrings

For the necklace:
8 ceramic donuts
2 spacer beads
27 gray cube beads
42 blue round beads
4 long gray beads
56 x 4 mm purple beads
2 cones
6 ft (180 cm) thread
1 card 0.8 wire

For the earrings:
2 donuts
2 blue round beads
2 gray cube beads
6 x 4 mm purple beads
0.8 wire
2 x 1½ in (38 mm) eyepins
1 pair earwires

round-nose pliers
necklace pliers
scissors

T hese ceramic beads from Greece come in soft, mottled colors. You could just wire one of the "donuts" and wear it on a thong, or you can make something really extrovert like the necklace shown here.

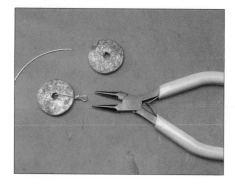

1 Wire the "donuts", as shown in the techniques section. Then cut three 2 ft (60 cm) lengths of thread and plan the beads and donuts onto the threads, so that they hang well together.

2 Take the threads through the spacer beads when you are happy with the design.

3 Bring all the threads through the beads on the side pieces.

4 Crimp the end of each of the threads, making a small loop. Then cut a short piece of wire, make a loop on its end, and hook the ends of the threads into this loop. Put the cones over the wire and turn another loop to attach the fastener.

5 The earrings are made by wiring the "donuts" and attaching an eyepin to the wire for the top beads.

fish chains
and earrings

For the chains:
10 fish beads
14 fish-shaped beads
24 x 2 in (50 mm) eyepins
28 x 1 in (22 mm) silver-plated swivels
¾ in (2 cm) 1.2 silver-plated wire
59 x 3 mm silver-plated balls
11 in (28 cm) silver-plated chain
31 x 0/7 gray rocailles

For the earrings:
6 fish-shaped beads
6 x 2 in (50 mm) eyepins
22 x 3 mm silver-plated balls
12 x 0/7 gray rocailles
6 x 12 mm silver-plated swivels
2 x 7 mm jump rings
1 pair earwires

TOOLS ETC:

round-nose pliers
wire cutters

*T*his is a very cheerful piece of jewelry, with lots of blue ceramic fish and fish-patterned beads swimming around your neck. They are even linked with swivels that are actually made for fishing tackle and then silver-plated for jewelry use.

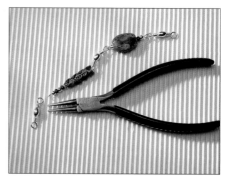

1 Make the straight pieces with the fish beads and fish-shaped beads on the eyepins. Arrange the silver-plated balls and rocailles around these beads.

2 Link the pieces together with the swivels by gently opening the loops on the eyepins sideways.

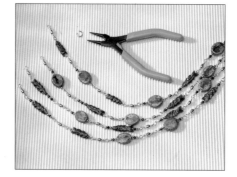

3 Lay the four lengths of chain and beads together to make sure that the lengths and arrangements are right. Make a large jump ring, as shown in the techniques section, for each end and connect the necklace together.

4 Add a piece of chain to each end, and make a hook for one of the ends. This is shown in the techniques section.
The earring beads are put onto eyepins and then hung from the smaller swivels, and put onto jump rings and the earwires.

charm
bracelet

4 copper-plate fish
1 brass elephant
6 x 8 mm copper beads
2 x 15 mm decorated
copper-plate beads
26 x 4 mm pale purple
beads
23 x 3 mm gold-plated
balls
13 x 2 in (50 mm) gold-
plated eyepins
2 x 7 mm gold-plated
jump rings
1 gold-plated fastener
13 links of brass chain
(from a hardware store)

round-nose pliers
wire cutters

T his is a very jolly collection of brass chain and brass and copper beads.
We have made a really musical charm bracelet with fish and elephants.

1 Make the hanging pieces for the
bracelet using the beads, balls, and the
fish and elephant beads, clipping off any
excess length on the eyepins and turning
loops at the top.

2 Open the loops sideways to hang
these pieces from the chain.

3 Put the fastener onto the chain with the
jump rings.

rainbow collar
and earrings

For the necklace:

17 x 1½ in (36 mm) rainbow drops

14 x ¾ in (20 mm) rainbow drops

26 x 5 mm round beads

62 x 0/7 black rocailles

27 x 2 in (50 mm) eyepins

1 ft 4 in (40 cm) silk thread

2 calottes

4¼ in (11 cm) chain

1 ready-made hook or 1.2 wire

For the earrings:

2 x 1½ in (38 mm) rainbow drops

2 x 5 mm round beads

4 x 0/7 black rocailles

2 x 2 in (50 mm) eyepins

1 pair earwires

round-nose pliers
wirecutters
scissors
glue

It was suggested that this could also be called a Rasta necklace because of the predominance of colors. This is a very easy necklace to make, and it would never go unnoticed!

1 Put the drop beads onto the eyepins, clip off any extra length, and make loops at the top of them. Four of the smaller drops have rocailles, or round beads and rocailles, above them.

2 Make a knot at one end of the thread and put a drop of glue onto the knot, then put a calotte over the knot. Thread the beads and the beads on eyepins onto the thread.

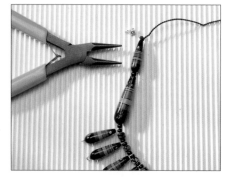

3 Again knot the silk at the end and put another calotte over the knot. Trim the loose ends of thread.

4 Add a piece of chain on one side of the necklace, and a hook to the other side, so that you can wear the collar at different lengths.

The earrings are simply put onto the eyepins with rolled ends.

AQM

accessories
and gifts

~

decorated
box

plain cardboard box
1 flat glass cabochon
450 x 7 mm bugles
1.5 g (0/7) gold rocailles

TOOLS ETC:

ruler
craft glue
crayon
large needle

Simple decorations make a plain box look opulent and exciting.

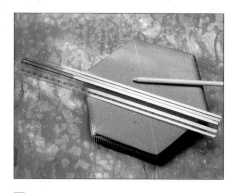

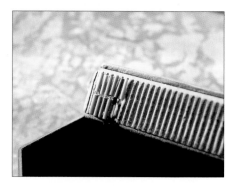

1 Mark the design onto the box lid.

2 Use craft glue to stick the beads onto the box. Start with the ridged sides. Put glue into some of the grooves and then put two bugles and a gold rocaille into each one.

3 Glue on the central glass cabochon. Then start gluing beads along the straight lines on your box lid. Use your needle to position the bugles with a gold rocaille between each one.

4 Spread more glue in the center of each triangular section. Position a few more bugles in these sections. Sprinkle the gold rocailles liberally onto the rest of the glue. Now work on the other sections of the box. When you have finished the design, check the positioning of all the beads and leave the box to dry.

embroidered
blouse

a blouse
strong fine thread
beads – such as rocailles,
bugles, or other small
beads

fine needles

Y et again, we let the design on the item suggest the project to us! You could draw a design onto a garment and then embroider the beads onto that, as we have shown on our sample piece. Or you can choose something like the blouse illustrated, which already had a design on it, and was enormous fun to embroider.

 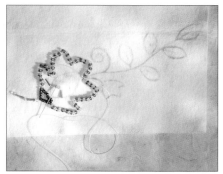

1 You could sew on individual beads using backstitch. Or you can work small sections by threading a few beads onto your pattern, and then bring your thread back through from the other side and catch your beaded thread to stop the beads from having too much movement.

If you were doing a very beautiful piece of bead embroidery, you could use couching. To do this, you have your beads on one thread, and use another thread to come from below between each bead to secure them.

Don't forget to use only beads that can be washed if you are embroidering with them.

bead

curtain

1 ft 4 in (40 cm) angled
doweling

29 x 4½ ft (35 cm)
polyester thread

284 silver bugles

79 dark blue bugles

145 turquoise bugles

81 green bugles

28 x 5 mm faceted beads –
light blue

32 x 5 mm faceted beads –
green

34 x 5 mm faceted beads –
dark blue

14 x 6 mm faceted beads –
light blue

c 600 x 0/7 rocailles

c 60 french crimps

wood stain, or
permanent marker
pen
fine needle
scissors
necklace pliers
awl

You can use beads to great effect as a window decoration. It is sensible to choose reasonably inexpensive beads, since even a small curtain will require a lot of beads. The effect is very rewarding. We give dimensions and numbers of beads for the curtain illustrated, but if you want a different-sized curtain you will obviously need to adjust these.

1 Cut the piece of wood to length and make sure that it does not have rough ends. Then stain it. We used a permanent marker pen, so you could stain to a color to match the beads, or your room.

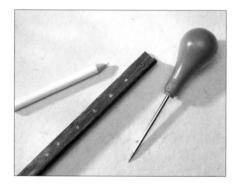

2 Figure out how many strings of beads you are going to hang and measure along the top of your wood. Then make holes through the wood with an awl.

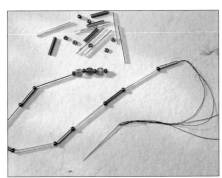

3 Thread one rocaille into the middle of your pieces of thread, to hold the beads at the bottom, then thread double through the other beads.

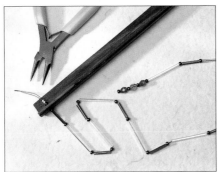

4 Bring the threads up through the wood and put two crimps onto the top of the threads to hold them in place. The crimps will be hidden by the angled wood. Hang the curtain from right-angled hooks.

spider's web
hat

a hat
rocailles
bugles
10 mm round flat beads
small hearts
thread

needle
scissors

T*he hat was already interesting, but the design of it seemed to ask to have beads added and, of course, they ended up like a spider's web. The strings of beads have been left loose on the hat, so that the movement becomes part of the design. The sample piece is shown flat for clarity and shows how you could add stripes in beads on a plain hat. We have not given precise amounts for the beads, as every hat (and head!) is different.*

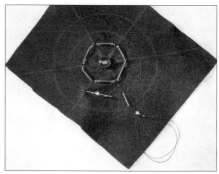

1 & 2 The sections of beads are strung onto the thread and then a small stitch is made to attach that section to the hat. If your hat has a lining, open a small section, so that you can work from both sides. You can then restitch it later.

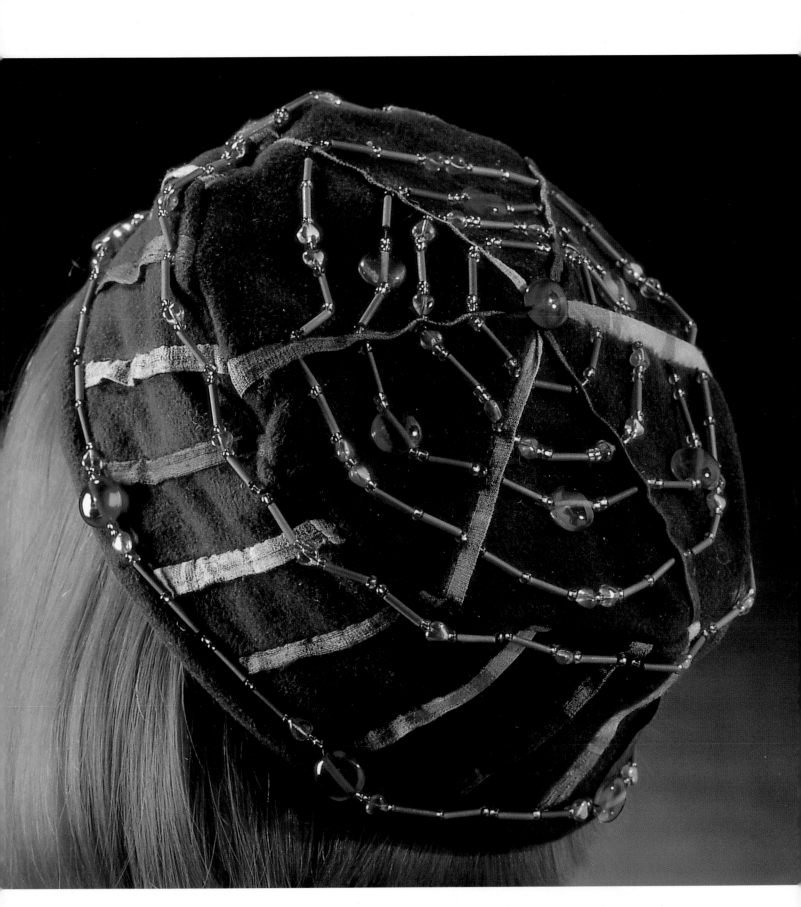

hat
band

YOU WILL NEED:

about ¼ oz (20 g) each of
three colors of the 3 mm
beads
1 x 10 mm bead for the
rosette
polyester thread

TOOLS ETC:

fine needle
scissors
glue

I f you do not want to have beads all over your hat, another good idea is to make a hat band with beads. We have used glass beads with a lovely sheen to them and worked a Peyote stitch to weave them together. This does require patience, but the band looks stunning.

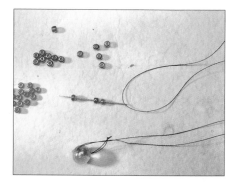

1 Cut a 5 ft (150 cm) length of thread, knot the end, and work it double through the large bead. Thread on one each of red, green, and blue beads in sequence, repeat four times, and pick up the knotted end of the thread to hold the beads in place.

2 Work on from here, threading red into red, etc. for five rows, making a rosette around the large bead. Leave the end of the thread in place.

3 Thread red, green, and blue beads onto a new long thread and then thread back into them with the same color so that you make a spiral of beads. Keep working in this way until you have created the right length for your hat, with the rosette between the two ends. The spiral of beads will be quite stretchy, so make sure it does not get too long. When you knot on a new thread, it is a good idea to put a drop of glue onto the knots as the polyester is very slippery. Always try to avoid getting glue on the beads.

4 Use the thread at the end of the spiral to weave through the rosette to join them, then use the loose thread from the rosette to work into the beginning of the spiral to join the circle completely.

curtain
tiebacks

polyester thread
an assortment of beads

strong needles
scissors

When we saw these tiebacks, we felt that they needed some beads! Again, the ones that we show here should only be considered inspirational, as you will find different tiebacks, and your color schemes will be different.

1 For the top of this tieback use rocailles to "anchor" the big rust-colored beads, making them rather like exotic fruits.

2 Beneath the rust beads are natural wooden beads, with a rocaille on each side of them. Think here of the positioning so that the beads are evenly spaced.

3 The final section has black glass beads sewn into the little loops on the tiebacks.

frame

YOU WILL NEED:

1 picture frame
100 x 4 mm purple beads
100 x 0/7 gray rocailles
40 x 0/8 green rocailles
15 x turquoise bugles
fine black polyester
thread

TOOLS ETC:

strong glue
needle (to move
beads)

*T*his is an easy way to make more of a plain frame. The colors of the beads gave the idea for the bunch of grapes design, but the scope is enormous, and you could really let yourself go with ideas for decoration.

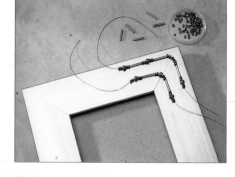

1 You could either make your design on paper first, or just arrange the beads onto the frame and then move them off a piece at a time to add the glue.

2 The bugles are best threaded onto short pieces of thread to glue them into place. When the glue is dry, you can remove the pieces of thread.

ACKNOWLEDGMENTS AND SUPPLIERS The Publishers are grateful to the following suppliers for their help and cooperation.

BEAD SHOP
43 Neal Street
Covent Garden
London WC2H 9PJ, UK

HOBBY HORSE LIMITED
15–17 Langton Street
London SW10 0JL, UK

LONDON BEAD COMPANY
25 Chalk Farm Road
London NW1 8AG, UK

BEADS (retail only)
259 Portobello Road
London W11 1LR, UK

CREATIVE BEADCRAFT LIMITED
Denmark Works
Beamond End
Nr Amersham,
Bucks HP7 0RX, UK

JANET COLES BEADS LIMITED
1 Shire Business Park
Wainwright Road
Worcester WR4 9WS, UK

BEAD SOCIETY OF GREAT BRITAIN
Carole Morris
1 Casburn Lane
Burwell
Cambs CB5 0ED

BEADWORKS
139 Washington Street
Norwalk,
CT 06854, USA

PERUVIAN BEAD COMPANY
1601 Callens Road
Ventura
CA 93003, USA

CREATIVE BEAD IMPORTS
255 South Terrace
South Fremantle
Western Australia

MAIL ORDER ONLY
(send a stamped addressed
envelope)

BOJANGLES
Old Cottage
Appleton,
Oxon OX13 5JH, UK

AHENZI
91 High Street
Winslow
Bucks MK18 3DG, UK

WORKSHOPS WITH
SARA WITHERS

Available through
OXFORD ARTS & CRAFTS
Gable end
Hatford
Near Faringdon,
OXON SN7 8JF, UK

DATE DUE

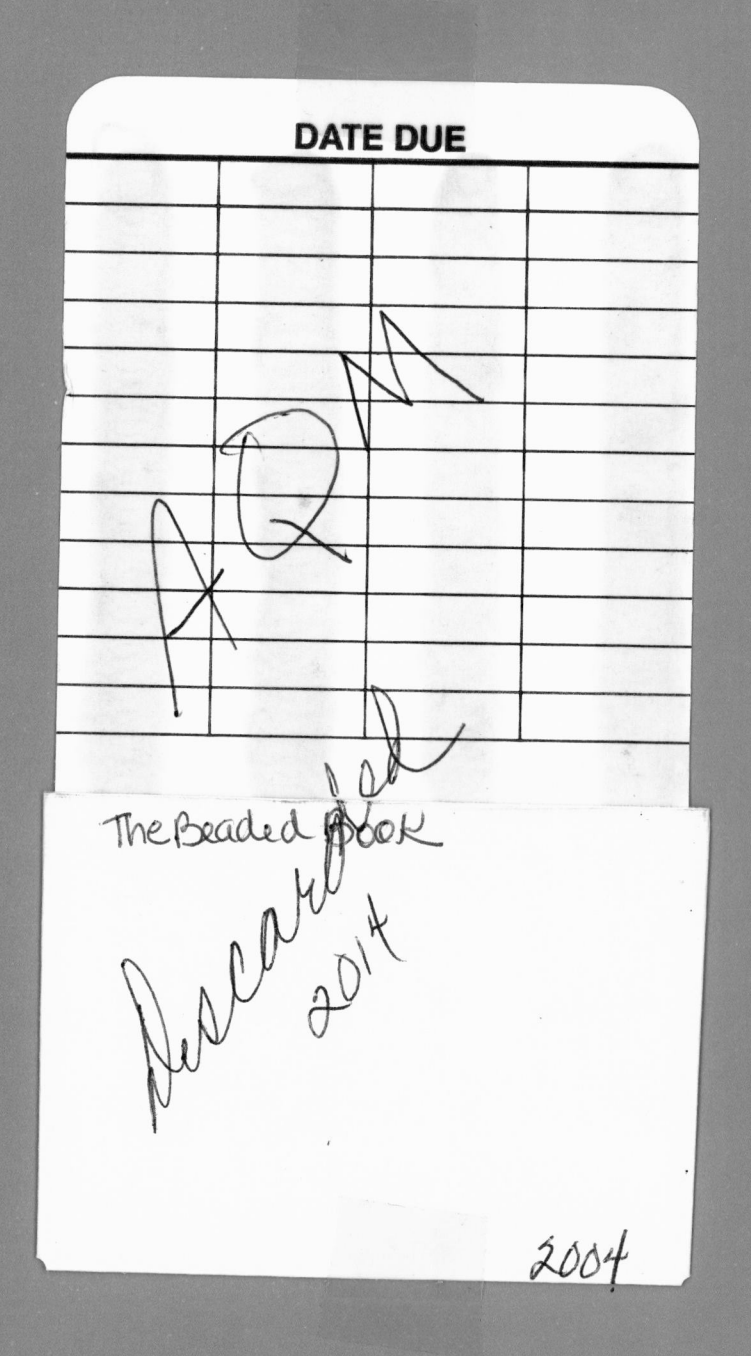

The Beaded Book

Discarded 2014

2004